Balance
Of
Nature

Balance Of Nature

ANGELINE LAN DOAN, O.M.D.

ARPress
ILLUMINATING IDEAS
EMPOWERING VOICES

Balance of Nature is translated from:
Can Bang Cua Thien Nhien
By
Angeline Lan Doan O.M.D.

ARPress
45 Dan Road Suite 5
Canton MA 02021

Hotline: 1(888) 821-0229
Fax: 1(508) 545-7580

Ordering Information:
Quantity sales. Special discounts are available on quantity purchases by corporations, associations, and others. For details, contact the publisher at the address above.

Printed in the United States of America.

ISBN-13:   Paperback   979-8-89389-558-2
              eBook   979-8-89389-559-9

Library of Congress Control Number: 2024920620

Table Of Contents

Respectfully Offered to My Parents:

Tuoc Van Doan
and
Mui Vuu (Anh Phung Vuu)

Dedication

Today we should apply this lesson of Vo Tuong (No Form) to our life. Establish a practical social ethics for the development of our own selves, of all people and of our country. Only then will we feel no fear for our survival. We should master our fear and we will be able to work for the creation of everlasting happiness and peace for us and for future generations. Paradise is within our reach provided we unite our minds and our hearts. The key to survival lies in our own hands. Whether it goes up or down, prospers or falls apart, the fate of this world will entirely depend upon all of us. "Living with a Kind Heart." To be able to live with a Kind Heart, we should know how to distinguish right from wrong, to judge things with wisdom, to deal with one another fairly. In family, community, or society, we should respect our elders and be tolerant to our juniors. To keep living with a Kind Heart is to pursue the good and avoid the evil. It also is our constant effort to improve ourselves physically and spiritually and set a good example to others around us. "Each person should attain a complete individual balance: absorb the neutral power between Yin and Yang and consequently achieve bliss on Earth." (Lisa Lan Doan/Angeline Lan Doan). Therefore, the highest direction for human beings is Humanitarianism. We help one another by sharing knowledge. We should treat others with true love and kindness. Only then can we find happiness in life. We should also perceive things with our heart. Use our heart to balance the knowledge of the mind. We know that the heart is the house of the spirit. The heart is like the moonlight and should be utilized to balance the sunlight, which is our brain. From Hindu literature we have these thoughts "The moon's crescent shape was perfect for an ideal resting place after the rigors of earth life." "Adore the sun, rising with all his rays, receiving the obeisance of Gods and demons, the shining maker of light." In conclusion:

The highest light can be seen as the creativity of the human brain and the benevolence and compassion of our heart. These lights are scientists, intellects, scholars and inventors in arts and technology. We should be grateful for the sunlight that has been giving us life and for scientists and intellects that make our future brighter. Good acts: striving for self-improvement and doing good things to society. Bad acts: being jealous and greedy, making wars to occupy lands and killing people or doing things that are counter to humanity. Let us have a look at countries on our earth. We can see the results of human actions. A country that is governed by good people enjoys peace and happiness. A country that is ruled by many bad people suffers from endless wars and famine. Therefore, today the world is also battered by a lot of serious diseases. There are Aids, all virus coming out, hepatitis, mental illnesses, and other medical problems without names. The scourge of wars has scared many of us. Our life is not safe because of deadly diseases.

My Deep Gratitude To:

Mr. and Mrs.
Heinz Haab - Christine Haab
Dr. Paul Tobler, M. D.

I am sincerely grateful to my friends for their wholehearted assistance
in the accomplishment of this book and especially to the translator:

Hoang Phuoc Ninh
Pham Xuan Thao

Art & Photo Designer:

Philip Le

Respectfully offering to and thanking:

My parents for the giving birth and upbringing. Heaven and Earth for granting me life and a creative mind. Our ancestors and sages for leaving a legacy of bright ideas and useful information for my instruction. Those who have been toiling to produce rice and other materials as well as providing me with ample means for every aspect in my daily life. Those who have contributed their thoughts about life for me to study. Those who have suffered and fallen.

And this path of life is dearly given to the young generations, to the elders and parents who are continually worried about our posterity's future.

Foreword

"I have known Dr. Angeline Doan O.M.D. for over three years now and the help she has provided me with has proven to be invaluable. When I began my treatment, I was mentally and physically exhausted. I had high levels of anxiety, a depressed mood all the time and trembling hands. Today I am back in college and am doing very well. The help Dr. Doan and her herbal remedy, the completion of her book and her high spirits lift everyone that comes into contact with her. Her book is very educational and is a joy to read. It conveys the love for life she has and her devotion for helping others. The book offers a hope for our future generations, gives us presently food for thought about how we treat one another, ourselves, and the earth we live on. Not only does she write about our bodies and how to take care of them, but she offers a spiritual path to follow as well. I enjoyed this book very much and will refer back to it to clear any kind of trouble I may have on my mind, to achieve "balance". I give my best wishes to all that have the pleasure of reading Dr. Doan's book. I highly recommend it and hope all have the same enlightening experience I have enjoyed."

Timothy Shaw

"Thank you, Dr. Angeline Lan Doan, for the privilege of reading **'BALANCE OF NATURE'**. Dr. Angeline Lan Doan describes various theories about herbal treatment, understandable human body. Balancing of YIN and YANG is the most importance of traditional treatment theory of oriental medicine in which Dr. Angeline Lan Doan focuses on her study and makes it helpful for readers. Dr. Angeline Lan Doan in her profession as a herbal specialist. Her research on the importance of herbal treatment reflects her professional skillfulness in serving people. I am honored and happy to be affiliated with her research."

Nguyen Viet Duc
State Employee of California.
Herbal nutritional healing (Vietnam 1975 –1978)
Nutritional Researcher, Vietnamese Food.

"Through the prism of Oriental philosophy, oriental medicine and oriental culture, Dr. Angeline Lan Doan has created this very important work, a masterpiece if you will. After studying and researching for very long time she has developed this book, in it a method of living. Dr. Doan wrote this book that after reading it, I found it a model of all virtues "pearl leaves and golden branches", for both conceptions of life and worldview. As a result of thinking continuously about life and having physical misfortunes of her own, she has rebounded from every set back. Constructed with the spirit materials and the philosophy and the medicine of the orient, Dr. Doan is ready to share her knowledge and experience with the world.

I cannot travel through all her philosophies in this forward, but in the contents of this book you will find teachings of Confucius; practices of charity and appreciating humanity. As will find in this book, Dr. Doan emphasizes balance of life as a key to good health and prosperity. She has developed her theory of truth, goodness, and beauty, which has reassured me as I read the book that these qualities can be obtained and practiced during all of our lifetimes. I am sure you will get as much out of this wonderful book as I have. Read and enjoy."

Dien Viet Duong

PREFACE

"Fate" is an ordinary term that contains something marvelous enough to cause our paths to meet today. I hope that my simple thoughts presented here will serve as the first steps to form our friendship. In order to share the optimal conditions that Mother Earth has lovingly provided us with, I wish to guide you on a tour to assimilate the spiritual food that I have had the wonderful opportunity to taste.

In our search of "The Truth, the Good and the Beautiful", we will have the occasion to join our hands to begin a close and dear relationship in an effort to achieve healthy, joyous, and bright life through these "golden paths."

Since I left Vietnam on April 9th of 1980 and came to Switzerland later on July 21, 1980, I have never stopped studying, applying, and realizing this precept: "Medicine and knowledge are to be used to save people."

I have chosen the work of saving people to be my vocation and have never forgotten my father's behest, "A good physician is like a good mother."

I arrived in a country, which is called "the Swiss paradise." Fate helped me to meet a man in this land, Mr. Heinz Haab. After only a short conversation we became very close. Incidentally this meeting would change the thoughts that I intended to apply to my future life. From "a state of war" my mind made a turn-about and achieved "a state of peace" radiate with beautiful and creative light that I am going to offer to you.

Another extraordinary feat brought me to the United States and then today thanks to Mr. and Mrs. Heinz-Christine Haab and Dr. Paul Tobler's advice, I am going to accomplish my work with this book.

This study is a synthesis of many parts I would like to share with you.

"Nutrition -Yoga, meditation for peace of mind - Exercise for a long life - Ascendant spirit."

I have learned a lot of useful things from various sources of information and knowledge in these countries during the past 18 years. But let us consider what is really necessary for our present life, what we want and what we have to do for it.

Do you think we truly need pure and nutritious food after many expressions and exchanges of ideas? I wish to share as well as offer you good food and delicious fruit that God and Mother Earth have been granting us, their beloved children.

This book is divided into three parts:

Share 1(Nutrition): Every one of us knows that food is important in everyday life, but we should learn to know that "Food is also medicine." Since it is an essential factor to sustain life, we must select the one that is pure and nutritious for our bodies. Basically, when we eat, we have to be moderate because abuse may result in indigestion. Our ancestors taught us "Eat to live and not live to eat." This teaching reminds us to keep a balance between moderation and needs in our diet. This is the method of nutrition for a long life. Please look for more information on nutrition on the following pages.

Share 2 (Exercise for a healthy and long life - Yoga, Meditation for peace of mind): Now I would like to share with you the second step in our search of a healthy life. All of us will agree that exercise can give us a beautiful body. It is also the basis that enables us to be healthy and have a long life. More information on exercise will be found on later pages.

Share 3 (Ascendant Spirit): Aiming at the good: In preserving life we need not only strength but also spirit because if "our spirit is lost, our body will perish." Concealed throughout the fabric of our life, there is an important fiber. It is our spirit. Ascension means we have to ennoble our existence with a beautiful spirit. Look for more information on spirit on the following pages.

SHARE 1: <u>NUTRITION</u>

Food is very important in our daily life. But food is also medicine.

Nature's law dictates that every species on earth - human beings, animals, or plants - each one in its own way has to eat to survive. The bottom line is how we combine our variety of food in such a way that best benefits our body and enables us to enjoy good health, beauty, and longevity.

Our ancestors had discovered this method of nutrition from the ancient days. They followed nature's Yin and Yang principle and selected only nutritious substances to fit and sustain their health.

<u>Moderation in Eating and Working</u>:

Ancient literature taught us: "Don't exert yourself too much; don't fluctuate your spirit, then you can enjoy longevity" or "Irregularity in working and resting or eating and thinking will certainly make you get hot in the head." These behests ask us to take care of both our body and our spirit if we wish to live to an advanced age.

Besides moderation we need to exercise continence in daily life.

<u>Continence</u>:

If we wildly indulge ourselves in sexual desires, our semen will be drained, our primary energy (Qi) dispersed.

But if we do the contrary, our bones will be solid and filled with marrow. Microbes and bacteria can only attack a weak person. But a strong body well protected by solid Qi is inviolable. Furthermore, we must know how to nourish Yang Qi in spring and summer, Yin Qi in autumn and winter because they are the basis of the Yin-Yang principle. However, we should be aware that Yang Qi is from Yin Qi and vice versa. Without Yang, Yin cannot be formed. Without Yin, Yang cannot be born. Similarly, when we grow a plant, we have to take good care of it roots by fertilizing and watering it properly and sufficiently.

Our ancestors had known how to tailor their macrobiotic method in accordance with nature's Yin-Yang principle, and thus enjoyed longevity. If we live contrary to nature's law, we will damage our vital energy and decrease our longevity. So, the important thing to bear in mind is that we have to follow nature.

"Spirit in peace, longevity will be attained.

Spirit in pieces, body will be ruined."

To live well requires us to observe these two factors:

- Nutrition: Our food needs to contain nutrients essential to good health and proper body development.
- Frame of mind: We should maintain moderation and self-restraint as taught in the following words by Lao-Tse:

"Being satisfied with your own condition saves you from shame. Knowing when to stop keeps you from danger and helps you last long."

I. NUTRITION:

Our body needs important nutrients to keep it in good shape. They are:

- Proteins
- Lipids (Fats)
- Carbohydrates
- Vitamins
- Minerals
- Water

These nourishing compounds, easily found in food, are essential to the production of energy for our body, its organs' functioning and its process of metabolism.

These nutrients come from:

- Various vegetables with green or yellow color
- Potatoes, fruit, and other vegetables
- Milk
- Poultry, meat, pork, beef, fish, eggs
- Cereals
- Butter and margarine

1. Proteins:

They are main materials that help provide antibodies, cells, and hormones for both human and animal bodies. Proteins are composed of amino acids linked in chains. We can find them in food of animal origin such as meat, fish, poultry, milk, and eggs.

We can also find proteins in such grains as soybeans, peanut, rice, corn, and fruit. But these plant proteins are found in smaller amounts than in food of animal source.

Our need for proteins may vary depending on our state of health.

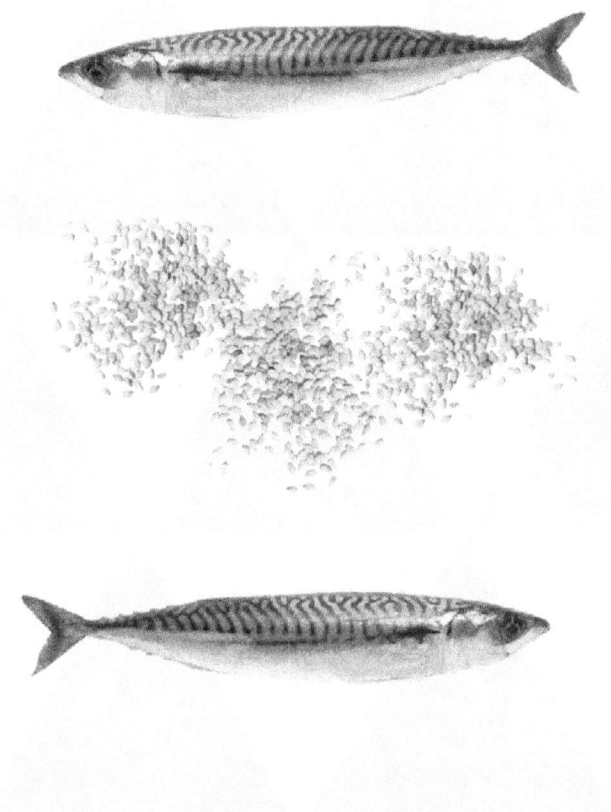

2. Lipids:

Lipids are fatty substances found in living things such as animal fat or vegetable oils.

Lipids do not dissolve in, but float on water surface.

Lipids include:

- Fatty acids, cooking oils and combined fatty substances.
- Glycerol
- Phospholipid
- Lipoprotein
- Cholesterol

In January 1990 the American Heart Association recommended that the daily intake of lipids and salt be kept at:

67 g lipids or less

22 g animal fats or less

3,000 mg salt or less

3. Carbohydrates:

These are organic compounds composed or 3 elements: Oxygen, Hydrogen and Carbon. They are classified into several forms:

- Uniformed sugars provide the main source of energy. They are glucose and fructose, which is found in ripe fruit.
- Dual-formed sugars includes Lactose (a sweet crystalline substance present in milk), Maltose (a sugar present in starches and malt)
- Sucrose: a sugar found in sugar cane, beet, carrot, and a variety of fruit.

  - Multi-formed sugars are composed of several simple-formed sugars. The most necessary of them fall into these categories:

- Cellulose
- Glycogen
- Starch

These produce DNA and RNA in cells of the body. Carbohydrates are basic elements that help the absorption of calcium and the fermentation in intestines. Lactose facilitates digestion, enabling the body to assemble natural bacteria in intestines to produce Vitamin K, etc.

Therefore, we should provide our body with sufficient daily need of carbohydrates. They are the main supplies of energy for the functioning of our body's six Fu and five Zang (internal organs).

Most importantly, glucose (blood sugar) provides essential energy to the working of the neurons of our brain and the other parts of the nervous system. Lack of glucose and oxygen can damage the brain or stop its functioning. A minimum of 9 to 11 mg of glucose is required for each cubic centimeter of blood.

These sugars are found in fruit, confections, cereals, milk, peas, and vegetables.

4. Vitamins:

Vitamins are substances necessary for our life. Except for Vitamin D, which is produced with the help of sunlight, and for some of Vitamin K, which is made by bacteria in the intestines, the rest is found in tiny quantities in all organic food.

Based on their effects, vitamins are classified as:

(1) <u>Vitamin A:</u> It is present in fish liver oil, liver, papaya, spinach, mango, tomato, milk, eggs, oranges, carrots, and other vegetables. Vitamin A can help us in the treatment of eye disorders. Lack of this vitamin may result in hepatitis. According to traditional Oriental medicine, liver is related to eyes and other skin problems. Lack of vitamin A can prevent growth of strong bones healthy teeth and the nervous system. However, abuse of this vitamin may produce toxic effects and diseases.

(2) <u>Vitamin B:</u> Consisting of B1 to B15, each kind of this vitamin helps our body to stimulate the growth of the nervous system, muscles, or red blood cells. Vitamin B also helps fix skin disorders, or beriberi. Normally, our body needs B1 to B9 and B12 the most.

   (a) <u>Vitamin B1 (Thiamin):</u> It is abundantly present in unpolished rice, beans, peas, and meat. If our body lacks Thiamin, it can be attacked by beriberi, neuritis, heart failures, and muscular paralysis and can result in death.

   (b) <u>Vitamin B2 (Riboflavin):</u> This vitamin aids in body growth, alleviates fatigue, produces red blood cells, regulates thyroid gland's activities and functions with other substances to metabolize fats, carbohydrates, and proteins. It is found in beef, fish (mackerel), green leafy vegetables, milk, and eggs. Lack of B2 results in chapped mouth or lips, glossitis, eye itching and other eye disorders.

   (c) <u>Vitamin B3 (Niacin):</u> This vitamin is water-soluble. It cannot be destroyed by light and heat or by acids and alkalis. The best natural sources of B3 are chicken, lean meat, peanuts. Lack of B3 causes loss of appetite, fatigue, pellagra, and indigestion, which can be harmful to liver. Overdose of Vitamin B3 may result in contraction of blood vessels.

(d) <u>Vitamin B5 (Pantothenic Acid):</u> It is necessary for maintaining normal growth and development of the nervous system and other body activities. Lack of B5 causes us to lose appetite and develop indigestion, depression, fatigue, low spirits, irascibility and sometimes loss of sense in our limbs.

Vitamin B5 can be found in liver, egg yolk, kidneys, or beef.

(e) <u>Vitamin B6 (Pyridoxine):</u> This vitamin helps the body regulate various steroids in our brain and nervous system and thus maintains the immune system.

Vitamin B6 can be found in nuts, meat, liver, beans, peas, or fish. Lack of B6 may result in anemia, depression, skin disorders like itching, and reduction of body resistance to illnesses. Overdose of B6 can cause temporary paralysis of certain nerves (symptoms will soon disappear as we stop taking B6).

(f) <u>Vitamin B7 (Biotin):</u> Besides the fact that some of it is formed in the intestines, this vitamin is present in egg yolk, beans, nuts, mushrooms, liver, milk, meat, and fish. Lack of B7 may result in weakness of muscles or myalgia, loss of appetite, dizziness, and oversensitive skin (dermatitis in children). Daily dose recommended for this vitamin is 100 to 300 mg.

(g) <u>Vitamin B9 (Folic Acid/Folacin):</u> This vitamin is the basic to form Vitamin B12 and Chlorine. It is essential to the formation of red and white blood cells in bone marrow. Lack of B9 may result in slow growth, anemia, stomach and intestine ailments, and mouth and tongue sores.

B9 is present in dark green leafy vegetables, liver, lettuce, and beans. Daily dose recommended for this vitamin is 400 mg.

(h) <u>Vitamin B12 (Cobalamin):</u> This vitamin is dark red. It consists of phosphorus, cobalt, and nitrogen. It is necessary for promoting body growth, maintaining a healthy nervous system, and regulating the functions of cells in intestines and bone marrow.

B12 is found in meat, fish, milk, eggs, liver, and kidney. Our daily need is about 3 micrograms for adults and 4 mcg for pregnant or nursing women.

(3) <u>Vitamin C:</u> Also known as Ascorbic Acid, it is essential to the formation of collagen that is important for the growth and repair of bones, body tissues and cartilage. Vitamin C helps heal wounds. It also aids in the treatment of neurasthenia or amnesia.

Collagen is produced to help our body form more steroids, get rid of toxins or medicine with strong reaction. It can also assist in the treatment of common cold. In over 10 years' clinical experience, the following prescription of mine has proven very effective in the treatment of viral flu or common cold:

- Squeeze one lemon and one lime for their juice.
- Honey (quantity depending on individual preference)
- A little table salt (sodium chloride) dissolved in 4 ounces of lukewarm boiled water.

Mix these three ingredients and drink 3 times a day when you have a cold or when you are under certain toxic effects. Remember that this prescription is contra-indicative for patients with stomach problems.

(4) <u>Vitamin D:</u> In nutrition, Vitamin D is an organic compound necessary for the development of our body. Under the effect of sunlight, the body can produce this vitamin. But we need to help our body especially when we are rarely exposed to the sun. This vitamin occurs in several forms, especially Vitamin D1 and Vitamin D5 and produced by ultraviolet radiation of sterols. Vitamin D is necessary for normal growth of bones and teeth. It can also:

- Help kidneys reabsorb phosphate and absorb into blood the quantity of calcium excreted from kidneys.
- Help assimilate calcium and phosphate into blood and intestines.
- Help develop muscles.

The daily dose recommended by FDA is 400 IU for adults. Lack of Vitamin D may result in rickets, deformed leg bones, small thorax, protruding forehead and osteomalacia.

Excessive intake of Vitamin D can cause kidney stone, brittle bone problems, abnormal calcium deposits in muscles and mental retardation.

Vitamin D is found in milk, fish liver oils, liver, and eggs.

(5) <u>Vitamin E:</u> This fat-soluble vitamin is necessary for our body functions. It can be found in cereals (wheat, malt), green leafy vegetables, vegetable oils and beans.

Vitamin E can help delay the aging process in our body cells. It can also reduce the weakening of muscles. Its scientific name is Tocopherol or Vitamin E Alpha-Tocopherol.

Lack of Vitamin E can damage red blood cells and cause bad effects on the nervous system. Overdose of this vitamin, however, may result in fatigue from blood pressure problems.

(6) <u>Vitamin K:</u>

Vitamin K has two forms:

- In leafy vegetables, tomatoes, eggs, soybean, liver, especially in green vegetables or spinach.
- Natural bacteria in the intestines can form Vitamin K.

Vitamin K promotes blood clotting, prevents internal bleeding, and helps heal injuries. Vitamin K of natural sources can be easily dissolved in water.

5. Minerals:

Minerals are inorganic elements that come from organic matters throughout the process of oxidation and are essential to the nutrition of human beings. Following are those required for our body's maintenance and functions:

- Calcium (Ca)
- Sodium (Na)
- Chlorine (Cl)
- Phosphorus (P)
- Magnesium (Mg)
- Potassium (K)
- Sulfur (S)
- Iron (Fe)
- Zinc (Zn) *
- Copper (Cu) *
- Cobalt (Co) *
- Manganese (Mn) *
- Fluorine (F) *
- Iodine (I) *
- Selenium (Se) *
- Chromium (Cr) *
- Tin (Sn) **
- Nickel (Ni) **
- Silicon (Si) **

- Vanadium (V) **

Notes:
* - Needed in small amount
** - Need in very small amount

The following are less important minerals that may enter our body:

- Mercury (Mg)
- Lead (Pb)
- Gold (Au)
- Silver (Ag)
- Gallium (Ga)
- Aluminum (Al)
- Bismuth (Bi)
- Lithium (Li)
- Strontium (Sr)
- Boron (B)
- Arsenic (As)
- Antimony (Sb)
- Beryllium (Be)
- Cadmium (Cd)
- Barium (Ba)

Minerals are essential to the equilibrium of Yin and Yang in our body. They control the alkaline-acid balance and keep the pH level in the middle to regulate the body's activities.

Minerals are also necessary for our sensory perception. They produce a Yin and Yang electric current through the movement of sodium and potassium resulting in a reaction that transmits signals through the nervous system.

Calcium and phosphorus: Calcium and phosphorus work together for the development of healthy bones and teeth. Phosphorus is also necessary for the proper metabolism of B vitamins. Calcium and phosphorus are found in milk, meat, fish, green vegetables, and beans. The daily need for our body is 800 mg to 1000 mg.

Iron: It is essential for the production of hemoglobin in red blood cells. These blood cells convey oxygen from lungs to nourish body cells, and then carry carbon dioxide from them back to lungs to discard it. Hemoglobin is produced and re-produced as blood cells in spinal marrow. Iron also helps regulate the respiration of cells and other nutrients for the production of energy. Iron can be found in liver, kidney, beef, egg yolk, grapes, green vegetables, and beans.

Copper: It is necessary for the proper working of red blood cells, the immune activities, for the benefit of the heart and the production of bones. It also helps with the metabolism of cholesterol. Lack of copper may affect children's healthy growth both physically and mentally, most obviously seen in the deficiency of pigment in the hair and skin (albinism). Lack of copper can also slow down the development of bones and may result in loss of consciousness.

Zinc: It is essential for the absorption of proteins, the formation of new cells and the proper development of red and white blood cells. It also helps regulate the pH level in our body. Lack of this metal can cause scabies, other skin problems, reduction of immunity, and hindrance in the normal growth of cells. It also slows down healing time for wounds. Zinc can be found in cereals, heart, liver, mutton, kidney, oysters, clams, and beef.

Iodine: The amount of iodine in a human body is about 20 to 30 mg. This mineral plays an important role in the work of the thyroid gland. This two-lobed endocrine gland is located in front and on either side of the trachea. Near this gland there are other smaller organs called parathyroid glands. The lack of iodine results in swollen thyroid gland, commonly known as goiter. In children, this problem can cause deafness, muteness, cretinism, and mental illnesses. Iodine can be found in seafood and seaweeds. Daily need for our body is 50 to 75 µg or 100 µg to 140 µg depending on age groups.

<u>Water:</u> Clearly, we cannot live without water. It is our most important nutrient. Lack of water can result in decrease of blood volume. If we lose 20% of the body water, we can die. A loss of 10% can result in serious trouble. We can lose 40% of our body weight and a majority of protein, sugar, or fat and yet we can survive. But if we lose much water, dehydration can cause fatal consequence. Water is the basic solvent for all the products of digestion and indispensable for the removal of wastes. Water also regulates our body temperature and our respiration.

Vital autonomic regulatory centers in the hypothalamus of the brain take care of the control of pressure adjustment and osmosis and make us thirsty. In a healthy body, the quantity of water taken in must be equal to that of water removed out of it within 24 hours.

Water is found in a variety of foods

- Fruit and vegetables contain about 90% of water.
- Meat: 60 to 75%
- Milk: 87%
- Dried fruit (bananas, grapes, pear, apple): 20%

Dehydration can occur because of perspiration or loss of fluid from diarrhea, vomiting and fever and can result in clonic limbs, brain damage and loss of consciousness. Moreover, the quantity of water in body must be adequate to maintain the acid-alkaline balance in the cells or the pH level. Without this balance, we may become victims to fatal epileptic seizures. Food rich in alkali (potassium, calcium, magnesium, and sodium) are milk, beans, nuts and especially almond. Those rich in acids (sulfur, phosphorus, and chlorine) are cereals, chicken, peanut, fish, and meat. Citrus fruit (grapefruit, orange, lemon) contain many organic acids that are good to keep our teeth healthy. Plums and apricots can produce acids in human body.

Our body must maintain the acid-alkaline balance to regulate the functions of its organs. If the intake of acid is too much, fainting can result. If there is too much alkali, fatal epileptic seizures can occur.

We need to keep:

- The pH level in the right amount to regulate the ion Hydrogen.
- The acid-alkaline to prevent the excess of electric charge from too much Hydrogen.
- Exhaling carbon dioxide (CO_2) from 1 to 3 minutes through the respiratory system.
- A good acid-alkaline balance through the work of the kidneys.

Regulation and balance of the pH level and discharge of hydrochloric, phosphoric, or sulfuric acids through transformation will bring about a healthy body.

II. SPECIAL CHAPTER: THERAPEUTIC DIETARY RECOMMENDATION FOR ANEMIA

In an effort to cure anemia, here are my ideas:

Anemia is defined in Dorland's Pocket Medical Dictionary as a "reduction below normal of the number of erythrocytes in the quantity of hemoglobin or in the volume of packed red cells..."

According to Western medicine, its symptoms include overeating, sudden body temperature rise, weight loss, edema, and hair loss. Of the thirty-three types of anemia, this chapter will address only the two most common kinds:

- Aplastic anemia is defined as the kind of anemia, which is resistant to therapy and characterized by the absence of regeneration of red blood cells.
- Iron deficiency anemia is defined as a form of anemia characterized by low or absence of iron stores, low serum iron concentration, low transferrin saturation, low hemoglobin concentration or hematocrit and hypochromic, microcytic red blood cells (See "Weak Spleen Yang and Kidney Yang")

Traditional Oriental medicine divides each of these two types of anemia into two sub-categories:

(1) Aplastic Anemia:

(a) Qi (Energy) and Blood Insufficiency:

- Clinical manifestation: pale or sallow face, dizziness, shortness of breath, trepidation, loss of appetite, light-colored tongue with a thin white coat, unsteady and weak pulse, forgetfulness and having nightmares if heart has been affected.

Treatment plan: Tonify Qi and nourish blood.

(b) Weak Spleen Yang and Weak Kidney Yang:

- Clinical manifestation: pale face, cold hands and feet, fear of cold, over-perspiration, weakness or pain in knees and lower back, weak voice, weakness in arm and leg muscles, bloated stomach, loss of appetite, vomiting, borborygmus, diarrhea, pale tongue with thin film; deep, slow, and weak pulse.

Treatment plan: Tonify Kidney Yang and Spleen Yang to improve transformation and transportation of food and fluids in patients' bodies.

(2) Iron-deficiency Anemia:

(a) Weak Spleen Qi:

Clinical manifestation: Abdominal pain, chest bloating, belching, nausea, diarrhea, loss of appetite, pale face, pale tongue with thin white coat and weak pulse.

Treatment plan: Tonify spleen and stomach Yang. Relieve abdominal distention due to cold and dampness.

(b) Qi and Blood Deficiency

Clinical Manifestation: (See "Aplastic Anemia")

Treatment plan: Tonify Qi and nourish blood in patients' bodies.

The first principle in treating "Weak Spleen Qi" or "Weak Spleen Yang" is to avoid foods that cool the middle of the abdomen (stomach). Foods that tonify and warm the middle of the abdomen is recommended. Any iced, chilled, or frozen foods should be avoided. Liquid foods should be taken in small amounts only when thirst occurs. All foods should be cooked and served hot or at least at room temperature. Raw foods should not be eaten at all.

The following foods are recommended:

- Meat/Proteins: chicken, turkey, beef, black bean, egg yolk, mutton...
- Vegetables: carrots, sweet potatoes, potatoes, squash, gourd, pumpkin, turnip, sleek, green onion, chestnut, scallion, pea
- Grains: sweet rice, oats
- Fruit: peach, cherry, strawberry, Chinese jujubes
- Herbs/spices: dried ginger, cinnamon, black pepper, cardamom, nutmeg, caraway, clove, coriander, star anise, garlic, ginseng, walnut, dill seed...
- Sweets: honey, molasses, barley malt, rice malt, rice syrup.
- Yellow-colored foods, well-cooked grains, small amount of meat and proteins, small amounts of well-cooked foods mentioned above. Herbs and spices may be used when cooking.

White sugar, lettuce, foods with too much liquid or too much sweet, raw foods, cold herbs and foods should be strictly avoided.

The treatment in Weak Spleen Yang and Kidney Yang is to warm both the Spleen and Kidney. This principle is similar to that of treating Spleen Qi or Weak Spleen Yang. Cold foods and excessive fluids should be avoided. Foods must be warm and eaten regularly in small amounts. Large meals should be avoided because they may result in indigestion.

To conclude, anemia is usually the result of spleen and kidney imbalance since blood is the product of combined energies from the spleen, kidney, and lung. Once again, the tonification and warming of the Middle Warmer (Stomach) is mandatory in treating anemia and the therapeutic principles for Weak Spleen Qi, Weak Spleen Yang and Weak Kidney Yang are applicable in addition to blood tonifying foods and herbs to the above-mentioned foods.

The following recipes are the author's original creative cuisine. The selection of foods was aimed at building energy and increasing appetite. The foods in the recipes are generally tonifying, warming and will directly help the Spleen and Kidney

Recipes:

Grains:
Sweet rice and chestnuts
12 dried chestnuts
1 cup of sweet rice
a little salt

- Soak chestnuts in water for 8 hours.
- Rinse them thoroughly.
- Place them in a ceramic crock.
- Rinse the sweet rice clean and put into the crock. Add 2 1/2 cups of water and a little salt.
- Put the crock in a pot and steam-cook for about 40 minutes to 1 hour.
- Serve black bean stew over sweet rice with chestnuts in a large bowl and garnish with scallion or garlic.

Effects of the ingredients:

- Chestnuts: sweet, warming, tonifying kidney, spleen, and stomach
- Sweet rice: sweet, warming, tonifying lung and stomach
- Garlic: pungent, warming, tonifying liver, kidney, and stomach
- Scallion: pungent, warming, tonifying lung, large intestine, and heart

Soup:

<u>Clove spiced sweet potato soup</u>
6 sweet potatoes
1/2 cup of walnut pieces
3 hard-boiled egg yolks
15-20 clove

- Peel and cut sweet potatoes into chunks and place them in a deep saucepan.
- Add 15-20 pieces of clove and water.
- Cook slowly for 2-3 hours, add water and mash potatoes into creamy consistency.
- Serve in a soup bowl and garnish with crumbled hard-boiled egg yolk and a sprinkle of crushed walnuts.

Effects of ingredients:

- Potatoes: Sweet, neutral, tonifying lung, kidney, and spleen.
- Walnut: Sweet, neutral, tonifying lung and kidney
- Egg yolk: Sweet, neutral, tonifying kidney and heart
- Clove: Pungent, sweet, warming, tonifying liver, kidney, and spleen.

Veggie Dish:

<u>Radish and Gourd Veggie Dish</u>
3 radishes
1 gourd cut into small slices
1 tbsp. of dill seed

- Place dill seed and washed whole radishes into a deep saucepan, cover with water.
- Cook for about 1 hour.
- Steam cooks small slices of gourd for about 45 minutes.
- Peel cooked radishes and cut into bite-size pieces. Discard water and dill seed.
- Serve in dish, garnish to make it attractive.

Effects of ingredients:

- Radish: Sweet, neutral, blood tonic.
- Gourd: Sweet, warming, tonifying spleen, kidney, and liver.
- Dill seed: Pungent, warming, tonifying kidney and spleen.

Black Bean Stew:

1 cup of black beans
1 1/2 cups of sliced carrots
2 cloves of garlic
1/2 tsp. of coriander
2 tbsp. of olive oil

- Soak black beans in water for 8 hours.
- Rinse thoroughly and discard soaking water.
- Place black beans in a ceramic crock with 2 cups of water.
- Steam cooks the crock for 1 1/2 hours.
- While beans are being cooked, wash and prepare carrots.
- Heat olive oil in a larger skillet, add minced garlic clove and sear.

- Add cooked black beans and vegetables and cover with water (about 1 cup).
- Sprinkle mixture with coriander and stir well. Simmer mixture down to stew consistency, add more water if you like.
- Cook until vegetables are soft.

<u>Notes:</u> Instead of using water to make this stew, you can substitute it with herbal soup for anemia. There are a number of appropriate herbal concoctions available. Select the one suitable to the type of anemia you are treating and use the herbal soup (at least 1 cup) to replace water. Your stew will have twice the healing power.

Effects of ingredients:

- Black beans: Sweet, neutral, tonifying kidney and spleen
- Carrots: Sweet, neutral, tonifying spleen
- Garlic: Pungent, warming, tonifying lung, spleen, and stomach
- Coriander: Pungent, warming, tonifying lung and spleen
- Olive: Sweet/sour, tonifying Qi and blood.

Dessert:

Delicious Chinese Jujube dish
1 cup of dried Chinese jujubes
1/2 cup of softened butter
1 1/4 cups of brown sugar
2 chicken eggs
1/2 cup of walnut pieces
1 tsp. of baking powder
1 1/3 cup of pastry flour
1/2 tsp. of vanilla extract
1/2 tsp. of table salt

- Cook jujubes in about 1/2 liter of water over low heat for about 15 minutes.
- Discard cooking water and cut jujubes in pieces. Preheat oven to 350° F.
- Use an 8"x8" baking pan.
- Mix butter with sugar and 1 cup of flour in a large bowl.
- Bake for 25 minutes or just until layer is golden brown.
- Meanwhile, mix jujubes with brown sugar, 1/3 cup of flour and the remaining ingredients.
- Pour the mixture over the baked layer.
- Bake for 25 more minutes.
- Let the cake cool and then cut it into squares and serve.

Effects of ingredients:

- Chinese jujubes: Sweet, warming, tonifying spleen and stomach
- Butter: Sweet, warming
- Brown sugar: Sweet, warming, tonifying spleen and liver
- Chicken egg: Sweet, neutral, tonifying Qi and blood
- Walnut: Sweet, warming, tonifying kidney and lung

There is an ancient saying that goes "medicine and food come from the same source." This demonstrates that for many years good food has delighted not only patients but also all of us and our families. Good food can heal and keep our bodies healthy. It can also bring us together socially and benefit our minds and feelings immensely.

SHARE 2: EXERCISE FOR A HEALTHY AND LONG LIFE YOGA - MEDITATION FOR PEACE OF MIND

It goes without saying that exercise helps blood circulate better in our body. It helps build or maintain strength and makes the body healthier. Exercise has both physical and psychological benefits to us.

Speaking of exercise for good health and longevity, we cannot ignore Yoga and its breathing techniques because of its crucial importance.

I. WHAT IS YOGA?

According to some research, Yoga can be understood as:

A way of meditation to achieve peace of mind. In time of depression, frustration, and suffering, we practice some form of Yoga in hope of achieving peace of mind and relaxing our spirit.

A martial art that helps build a sturdy body and get it ready for fighting against one's enemy. In this context, Yoga also means "Triumph over one's enemy."

A subject of learning in Buddhism.

Then, what does Yoga mean?

"Yo" in Yoga means "the light of an extremely beautiful stone". It is the symbol of brightness, merit, and good luck. It is also the combination of these qualities.

Spiritually speaking, Yoga is a path leading from a depressed and impure mind to a transcendent and pure one. It is the synthesis of the visible and the invisible, the limited and unlimited, and the atom and the cosmos.

A lonely, depressed mind only exists in an individual who lacks true love. Children are angry and upset with their parents because there is a big gap in the communication of their feelings. We are sad because we cannot associate ourselves with joy. Happiness and unhappiness are only mental products. Outside scene in itself is neither sad nor joyful. It is so only because of the state of our mind.

The Yogi (practitioner of Yoga) must use Yoga exercise to achieve a mind clear and moderate, a heart kind and loving to everybody and everything, and to build a body strong and healthy enough to overcome any lustful temptation and material test around him.

This is only a part of Yoga's definition. If we combine the term "yoga" with other terms, we will have different meanings.

Yoga has many schools. Each of them has different techniques of training. But they can be included into 6 major disciplines as follows:

- BHAKTI YOGA
- RAJA YOGA
- HATHA YOGA
- KARMA YOGA
- MANTRA YOGA
- JNÁNA YOGA

1. BHAKTI YOGA:

"Bhakti" means "Love". It is the guiding spirit of this discipline. It teaches us to respect and worship Gods or all Superior Beings.

It also teaches us to love one another and to take care of one another as we do to ourselves. We are taught to merge ourselves in one another's happiness and suffering if we wish to understand this love thoroughly. When we engage ourselves in everyday life, we can share these states of feelings that have been happening again and again over the course of time and space.

2. RAJA YOGA:

"Raja" means "Royal". It also means wealth and greatness. This is the technique that the Buddha used to concentrate and achieved peace of mind. This technique had its origin in Greece many years before the Christian era. It was spread to other countries about six centuries B.C. and then came to the valley Shindu. Lord Sakyamuni later modified this technique and used it to attain Buddhahood. Raja Yoga was also used by other religions, such as Hinduism.

In Buddhism, this teaching consists of Samadhi, Vipassana, Samatha. This Raja Yoga is known as meditation.

3. HATHA YOGA:

Hatha is a Sanskrit term. "Ha" means "Yang" and "sun". "Tha" means "Yin" and "moon".

Ha and Tha are always present in our body. Hatha Yoga helps us maintain the Yin-Yang balance in our internal organs as well as in our breathing.

"In Yin there is Yang and in Yang there is Yin". Such is the law of nature that enables every species to survive in the universe. With the Yin-Yang balance in the body, we feel good and healthy. We love and appreciate life. As a result, we can live a longer life.

Hatha Yoga is aimed at regulating every organ in the body while many kinds of other exercise serve primarily in developing various muscles.

The Yin-Yang balance helps us to find that life is worth living. It makes our thinking clearer, our mind brighter, our body sturdier and our life more valuable.

When we have a strong and healthy body, we want to live. Therefore, Hatha Yoga helps us become physically and mentally vigorous.

4. KARMA YOGA:

"Karma" means "actions and reactions" or "causes and effects" resulted from one's activities.

Actions are crucial in this technique. Of course, we have to always do good things that will help not only ourselves but also other people around us. We cannot do things for personal gains because these may harm others, the whole community or even society.

A Karma Yogi (one who practices Yoga) has to win over himself in any aspect, even to sacrifice his body and his career for the benefits of other people or other species.

On a broader range, this virtue had been exemplified by leaders of Christianity, Buddhism and by Mahatma Gandhi... From their lives and teachings, they left us many practical lessons. Under any circumstances, if we can do good things or invent anything that helps bring about more prosperity or more happiness to other people, we are indeed practicing the virtue of Karma Yoga.

5. MANTRA YOGA:

This technique is also known as Laya Yoga. It calls for the formation of sacred sounds (Mantra) or secret words with the assistance of Holy Beings to gain supernatural power and body. Yogis of this discipline are said to possess the capability of evicting evil spirits and of healing rather than liberating themselves.

6. JNÁNA YOGA

(Knowledge, wisdom, and intellect)

Jnána Yoga is a very difficult practice. It requires its followers to have very high intelligence to interpret or discover causes or reasons for every event or phenomenon.

A falling leaf, for example, can bring a Jnána Yogi to the exertion of his whole wisdom to try to answer such questions as: Why is the leaf falling? Where was it from? Why is it falling down and not up?

When we have understood the causes, we will not be uneasy or foolish anymore. Then we can realize the truth of nature or the universe.

According to Buddhism, this is the method practiced by its sages and enlightened ones. In early times when Buddhism and Christianity had not appeared, many sages had used their intelligence to observe and tried to find the light to show them the way in life through sounds and solitude.

I, myself, have had the good luck to be educated and trained by my grandparents and parents in the practice of most of these yoga techniques. Now I would like to contribute my small part in the hope of helping you, my dear readers, and our society to acquire the above-mentioned virtues.

On the following pages, I wish to share with you the beneficial path of the yardstick of Yoga (or the Direction of Yoga) that I have been taking all my life.

II. THE YARDSTICK OF YOGA

(The Direction of Yoga):

We believe that love is the basis of actions for a good person with a healthy body (Hatha Yoga mentions "Body") and a clear mind (Raja Yoga mentions "Spirit"). Yoga is not a religion. Therefore, it does not deal with only one physical or one spiritual aspect.

With a practical goal of improving our fate, we should use all our helpful discoveries as well as progress in our own thoughts and actions to serve ourselves and our world. Yoga helps us avoid factionalism or individualism and attain our supreme goal of "the Good" and "the Beautiful" in humanity's life. Yoga does not contain any political doctrines or any prejudiced beliefs to render you one-sided or interested only in your own cause. Yoga does not incur in you any fanatical dogmas in any shapes. Yoga shows us the need to exert our faculty of reasoning thoroughly to avoid superstition or fanaticism if we want to be called members of a civilized world.

For any yogi, good result of one's actions is very important because it is the yardstick of Yoga. In other words, it is the direction or guiding principle of Yoga. Beyond all limitations of nationality, race, religion or lifestyle, Yoga is essential to everybody. Yogis need to take love as the guiding principle of their actions and on a higher level, spread the compassion and charity of the Buddha and Jesus Christ, the benevolence of Confucius and the motherly love of the Holy Mother Mary and Kwan Yin (The Goddess of Mercy) to all men. This is called the sacred principle of Benevolence.

Love is the best way of healing and also the most effective tonic for human soul. A person who lacks Yoga is like a lamp without oil or a human without food. From the heart of the yogi flows an endless stream of love that sweeps away all individual prejudices and vanity and helps get rid of all bad customs or harmful practices that may destroy society and humankind.

Any leaders of religion or any sages should be proud of their posterity because they have kept themselves from being corrupted by pernicious habits and being able to control themselves. In short, a yogi is one who knows how to build himself a strong body, a clear mind, broad knowledge with compassion and sympathy for all to make the world happy on Earth. But Yoga is not an omnipotent god. It is only an antidote to superstition. Without it the road to evolution would be barred. Yoga is now widely studied in major universities in the world. Many students have adopted it to develop their bodies and souls. Raja Yoga brings us a cheerful, alert, and clear mind. Hatha Yoga brings us a strong and lively body. Thanks to Yoga, we are able to build a beautiful society, an eternal life with love as broad as an ocean, and solidarity as wide as the universe.

The Planet Earth that we are living on can be considered as a big tree of the cosmos. Each individual is a small universe. I am a leaf. You are the pretty flowers or delicious fruit. We exist in this cosmos-tree without regard to the color of our skin or hair because we are all humans. All species in nature: animals, plants without regard to their origins or differences are members of the same house.

III. BREATHING:

Although we need food to live, we can survive after 1 week or 10 days without eating. But if we do not breathe, we will be dead within 3 minutes except some experienced yogis who can withhold their breath longer.

Fresh air is essential to our breathing. Regular breathing will help blood circulate in our body. This is even more important to those who practice Yoga or physical exercise. Not only does breathing have a good effect on the circulatory system, but it also brings the joy to live, longevity and superb vigor.

I would like to say more about why breathing brings us vigor. In our body, there is Pranayama. According to Indian philosophy, the universe is divided into 2 parts:

- Akasha: Matter
- Prana: Energy

For each environment, there is a different structure. But there is nothing different in regard to matter. Today, science has demonstrated that lunar rock and earth rock have similar matter elements after studying the rock brought back from the moon by Astronaut Armstrong. Also, our solar system contains elements similar to those of systems that are millions of light years away from ours (the speed of light is 300,000 km per second).

Prana is omnipresent. Prana creates cosmos and everything. Prana is in the nucleus of an atom. Prana is not visible to naked eyes and always moving with electrons around it. The structure of Prana is similar to our solar system with Earth and other planets moving around the sun.

According to natural law, everything in the cosmos is created in the same way whether it is a solar system, an atomic nucleus, or a human body. When the cosmos disappears, Prana will operate in its different form waiting for its restoration to the former state when conditions favor. There will be a time when our Planet Earth comes to an end. After that it will be reformed into a new planet once Prana is combined with Akasha.

Prana has endless power. One who succeeds in controlling Prana in himself can control Prana in other people's bodies. He can also know things in the past and future. He is able to heal himself and others. These can be achieved because his mind is concentrated to a level that helps him know things, which are unsteady around him.

The ability to control and thoroughly understand Prana demands us, first of all, to gain the power from breathing. If we want to attract other people and become a famous person with exceptional talent, we need to have good breathing and good command of Prana in ourselves. We need to practice meditation through breathing techniques, Yoga, and basic physical exercise.

First of all, because breathing is very important, we have to learn how to breathe and get rid of harmful gases from the body. There are many breathing techniques. We can choose which fits us best. One of the purposes of breathing is to expel carbon dioxide from our body and increase the volume of oxygen in the lungs to reduce the risks of leukemia, liver and lung cancer and stroke.

This practice can also cure stress, a serious problem of our time. From my own experience, breathing has helped me achieve stability in body and mind after many adversities and recover after a lot of serious illnesses.

Here are two breathing techniques for you to choose from:

1. Breathing Technique 1:

You can do this before or after your work time, in flexible sessions (5, 10 or 20 minutes).

Practice: Look for a well-ventilated place with plenty of fresh air or a clean room with all windows opened about half an hour before practice. Focus your mind on nothing, without any sadness, worry, love, hate or anger. Then choose a position for breathing (4 positions: walking, standing, lying, and sitting.)

Let us begin after a specific position is already taken.

- Phase 1: Slowly, regularly and without any reluctance, breathe deeply in through the nostrils.

- Phase 2: Concentrate air to your belly at Dan Tian (Qihai-Ren. 6). Hold your breath. Practice to hold it for about 30 seconds to 1 minute depending on each individual's capacity. Exhale slowly through your mouth (lips closed with only narrow opening for air to escape). This breathing technique helps eliminate toxic gases such as carbon dioxide. Oxygen that is brought into your lungs will make your mind clearer and your body stronger. Regular exercise will develop your physical endurance, sharpen your reflexes, reduce your fatigue, and stress, and greatly increase your energy.

2. Breathing Technique 2:

Notion on the stages of the Qi (energy):

In the first phase of breathing, we need to concentrate to follow our breath. After a moment, we will feel a stream of heat accompanying our breath. This stream of heat is called the Qi of our body. Now we can direct energy to every part of our bodies. We can separate the Qi (energy) from the air we breathe. When we reach this level, we can stop breathing, and yet we can guide our Qi everywhere we want in our bodies.

The development of Qi can be described as follows:

- Our will can form energy with a stream of heat.

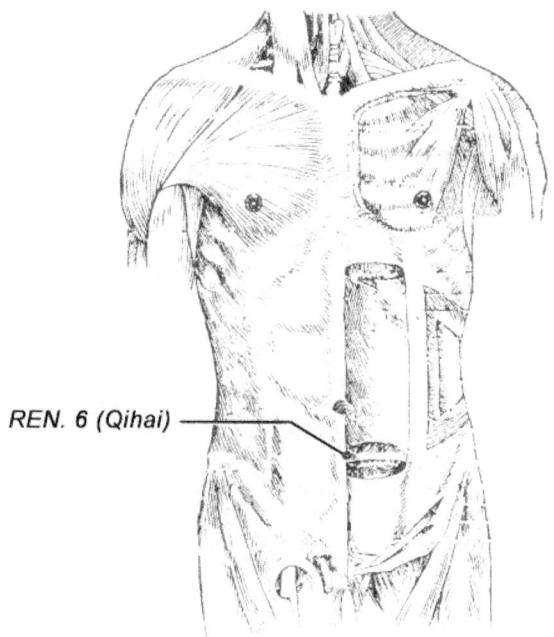

REN. 6 (Qihai)

- This stream of heat can give us power.
- Power can be turned into Qi.

When we can concentrate our breath to the highest level, we can generate Qi.

Preparatory steps for this technique are similar to those of Technique 1.

<u>- Phase 1:</u> Breathe in slowly through your nostrils. Concentrate air to the belly at Dan Tian (Ren 6) about 1.5 inches below your navel. Hold the air for 1 to 2 seconds right there.

Then from this position, bring the air upward along the spinal column to the waist and hold it there for about 1 to 2 seconds (point Du 4, Ming Meng Huo) (see drawing).

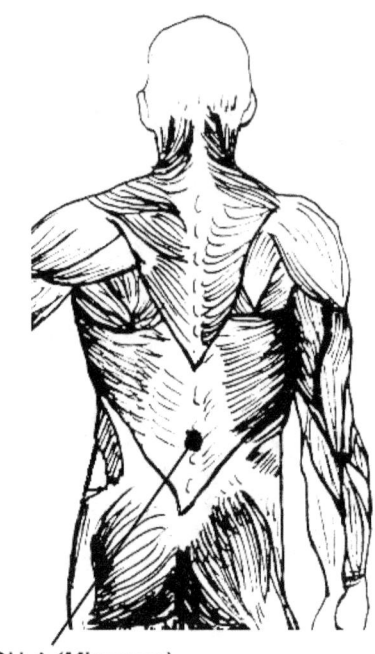

DU.4 *(Mingmen)*

Keep guiding the air upward to the neck (point Du 14, Dazhui) and hold it there for 1 to 2 seconds.

DU.14 *(Dazhui)*

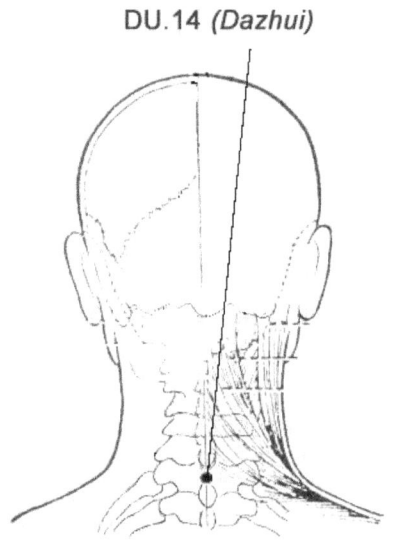

Bring the air toward the nape to the crown of the head at point Du 20 (Bai Hui) and hold it there for 1 to 2 seconds. From this upper position, bring the air downward between the eyebrows at point Yintang (see drawing).

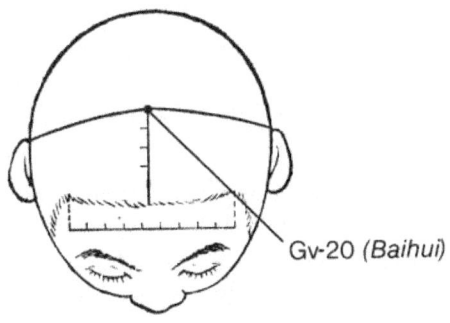

Gv-20 *(Baihui)*

Extra.3 (Yingtang)

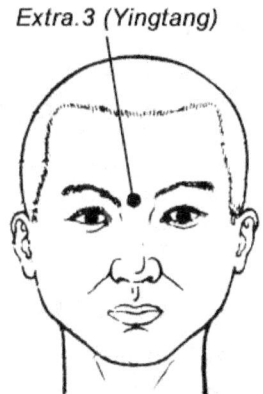

Hold it there for the last time. Then exhale through a narrow opening in your mouth. Phase 1 of breathing is thus completed.

- Phase 2: As you exhale, focus yourself to a specific point of your body; for example, the big toe on the right foot. Repeat phase 1: Inhale air, then concentrate it at Dan Tian (Ren 6) through the waist (Du 4, Ming Men), the neck (Du 14, Dazhui) and the crown (Du 20, Bai Hui). Hold your breath there from 1 to 2 seconds. Then exhale slowly downward to the right big toe.

- Phase 3: Bring air form the right big toe (in the above example) to the waist (Du 4). Hold it right there for 1 to 2 seconds. Bring it to the neck. Hold it there for 1 to 2 seconds and then take it to the crown. Hold it there for 1 to 2 seconds. From there bring your breath to between the eyebrows at point Yintang and hold it there for the last time before exhaling slowly.

Repeat these three phases for about 5, 10 or 20 minutes depending on your capacity.

The most important aspect of this breathing technique is that before you complete it, you have to concentrate your breath in the middle of your forehead at point Yintang.

This breathing technique promotes the elimination of toxic gases and thus protects our body form serious illnesses. It also enables us to increase our energy, maintain the Yin-Yang balance. The Qi (vital energy) concentrated at major points of the spinal column serves to stimulate the nervous system, accelerate the circulation between internal organs. Most importantly, this technique helps us open the seven chakras system in our body.

3. From Chakra 1 to Chakra 7:

This system includes major centers along the spinal column, in the brain and other points that control the circulatory system in various internal organs.

There are seven principal centers in the body:

Chakra 1: It is located in the spine and is associated with our survival. Its element is Earth.

Chakra 2: It is located in the lower abdomen and is associated with emotions and sexuality. Its element is Water.

Chakra 3: It is located in the Solar Plexus (Adrenals-Pancreas) and is associated with personal power and metabolic energy. Its element is Fire.

<u>Chakra 4</u>: It is located above the Sternum Thymus (Pulmonary and Cardiac Plexus: in the area of lungs and heart) and is associated with love. Its element is Air.

<u>Chakra 5</u>: It is located in the throat (Thyroid-Parathyroid) and is associated with communication and creativity. Its element is Sound.

<u>Chakra 6</u>: It is located in the forehead (Pineal-Carotid Plexus) and is associated with clairvoyance of intuition and imagination. Its element is Light.

<u>Chakra 7</u>: It is located in the crown of the head (Pituitary-crown chakra-cerebral cortex) and is associated with knowledge and understanding of oneself. Its element is thought.

To sum up, the seven chakra controls:

Chakra 1: Earth
Chakra 2: Water
Chakra 3: Fire
Chakra 4: Air
Chakra 5: Sound
Chakra 6: Light
Chakra 7: Thought, ideas

(Wheels of Life - Anodea Judith)

IV. EXERCISE:

We all understand that exercise makes us healthier physically and psychologically. Following are some major questions about exercise:

- What can be counted as exercise?
- A little exercise for a symmetrical body.
- How to lose weight with exercise.
- How much exercise is enough?
- Beware of exhaustion.

I would like to share with you these five points that I have been applying to my everyday life.

1. What can be counted as exercise?

We need not perform rigidly repetitive and forceful movements that may give us fatigue. We do not need special clothing. Any action or movement requiring the consumption of at least 4 to 5 calories per minute for an average person is considered effective exercise.

Activities such as housework, backyard gardening, ladder climbing, bicycle riding or dog walking, done in about 30 minutes, are considered sufficient exercise.

2. A litle exercise for a symmetrical body:

Everybody has his or her own needs. At the starting point of an exercise plan, if your body is unfit or not well proportioned, you need to strictly follow instructions aimed at getting it into good shape. In case your body is already physically fit, and you only want to sustain it, you can regularly follow an exercise schedule of 30 minutes per day for 3 days per week.

3. How to lose weight with exercise:

The best way to burn fat and calories is to exercise continuously for at least 20 minutes at one time. We need a long period of time to lose weight and we have to exercise for at least 30 minutes a day.

4. How much exercise is enough:

The experts until recently advocating "the more exercise the better" now withdraw this opinion. From my own experience, I have found that we need only 10 or 20 minutes for our daily exercise.

In other words, our health will be significantly improved if we exercise moderately and regularly rather than strenuously and irregularly.

Strenuous exercise may be done only by young people. Regular exercise is good for adults and the elderly to reduce the risks of heart disease, depression, high blood pressure, osteoporosis, and diabetes.

5. Beware of exhaustion:

Excessive exercise may cause exhaustion. Its signs are fatigue, low spirits, insomnia, and illness even when exercise is not being done. The extent of exhaustion depends on individual physical endurance and his health history. The important thing that we have to pay attention to when we practice any kind of exercise is the acceptance level of out body. Never overburden it with too much exercise. If we see that health is not improved, we should stop exercising. When we do run on a treadmill, bicycle riding and muscle building activity and reach the plateau of our endurance, we should put our practice on hold.

Take a break for a few days so that our body can rest. For exercise, quality counts more than quantity. Its goal is to give us health and a symmetrical body and not to over exercise and get ourselves burned out.

Ways to better your health and your fitness are innumerable, from Hatha Yoga to modern physical exercise methods, which are currently taught and practiced in fitness centers and universities everywhere. You have a lot of options tailored to your health and age. Try and choose which fits you best. But it is necessary for you to consult an expert before you make your choice.

SHARE 3: THE SPIRIT OF ASCENSION (AIMING AT THE GOOD)

Every one of us has his own knowledge and his own thoughts according to the state of his body and mind. In other words, the condition of his internal organs combined with the level of his knowledge will decide the quality of his own light. Simply put, a wholesome body with healthy organs and a profound and ascendant knowledge will give us a brighter light. But what can we do to obtain such a light?

In search of a light that will show us the way to a better life, I would like to share with you all the experiences gathered from my learning. I would also like you to understand my good will and forgive me if I make any mistakes because as we all know, "No man is perfect" physically and spiritually.

I wish that my light and yours would complement one another so that we can become better. This is also the way we contribute to serve our mutual purpose of creating perfect and more progressive life for mankind.

According to Oriental philosophy, our lives, as well as everything existing in this universe, from a nucleus to the cosmos are governed by the natural principle of Yin and Yang. The question is, "What can we do to gain a spiritually blessed and peaceful life in which happiness is guaranteed and shared by everybody."

First, we must build the "Yang" (Positive Attitude in our life). Why? Because with "Yang", we feel good, happy, optimistic, and thus likely to achieve longevity. But never forget to maintain the balance between Yin and Yang to avoid any excess that is beyond natural order. And why do we suffer from the imbalance? Besides well-being and happiness, we also need artistic harmony. Life can be compared to a musical masterpiece that matches its rhythms to the daily ups and downs of our existence. It can also be visualized as a superb painting whose mixture of colors makes our life more poetic and more magnificent.

To achieve this goal, we have to learn from the experiences of the sages of all times in human history. Please get acquainted with the wisdom of the great physician Hai Thuong:

"Yin's born when your spirit's calm,

Yang's stronger when you do exert your body."

Our spirit must be kept peacefully calm so that Yin can be born. Our body must be regularly exercised so that Yang can be strong and lasting. When our mind is calm, our nervous system is not agitated. Then our internal organs will be in good condition.

From ancient literature we have this behest, "Maintain your calm to nourish the true Yin." This teaches us not to overexpose our spirit. In other words, it means, "With excess of Yang, one tends to be joyful. With excess of Yin, one tends to be angry often." So, we ought to know how to control ourselves to maintain the delicate balance between Yin and Yang.

In nature, Yang is the generator of spring and summer. Yin is the repressing Qi (energy) of autumn and winter.

The image of Yang is fire. The image of Yin is water. Fire tends to blaze up, thus representing joy while water tends to flow down representing depression. Yang Qi is Heaven and Sun. If Yang Qi disappears or weakens, we cannot enjoy longevity.

Yang is the Qi of creation and procreation. Without Yang, Heaven will not be able to create all things or species. Without Yang, people cannot live just as the sky would become gloomy when there is no sun. When Yang is weakened, people will die young. Therefore, if we care for a long life, we need to protect the true Yang.

I wish that we could establish the true Yang as the foundation for our living environment while we aim at the good and Fine Arts so we can share a beautiful life with one another.

Sixteen years ago, on a beautiful Sunday morning, "Fate" led me to a charming little village with the name Lachen in Switzerland. There, a boy of about 16 to 17 years old approached me and said, "Ms. Lan, if you can answer this question in my school, you could become very rich, winning the Nobel Peace Prize and a reward from the European Union."

I asked Tuyen, the teenager, "What's the question?" The boy said, "The question that so far college and high school students in Switzerland cannot answer yet is: Suppose you are a politician, how could you develop poor countries around the world? Ms. Lan, are you able to bring forth a solution?"

Having heard the question, my mind was overwhelmed with exciting expectations. I thought that mankind now wanted to step closer to the True, the Good, the Beautiful and the true Yang.

One hundred fifty-five nations, including Vietnam, my own country, are classified as poor countries of the world. When we think of their poverty, we feel sorry, and we want to do something to help them. Politics are not my interest because many people have been abused in its name all over the world. What I would like to mention here is true politics, which comes from humanity's sincere benevolence.

I am a mere traditional Oriental medicine doctor and I do not have any political ambition. I only wish to find a practical way to help people. I have decided that it must be the way of a good physician. I wish I could follow the footsteps of Jesus or the Buddha and other saints in their spiritual way (the Tao of the Heart). I also would like to find the True Yang suitable to our time and helpful to all human beings. Back in Zurich, I kept reading and doing research to find the answer to the question that made me toss and turn in bed at night for three long months.

At last, I found the light to show the way in our own body. Our body has 365 points with different names and functions. Among the literature that I had read, the book by the great physician Hai Thuong helped me most in this discovery. I found out that our body holds a very secret and invaluable treasure that contains the illuminating philosophy about the True, the Good and the Beautiful.

I hope that these golden goals, which I am trying to follow every day, will be applied to our life.

The sacred value that I have been wholeheartedly seeking is not for the sake of any material remuneration from the people who had raised the above question, but for the sake of the true and bright humanness, which many people have intentionally or accidentally neglected. Even if I won the reward, my answer would not be of any help if I did not pay attention to the true problem of humanity. Those who had raised the question would be doing a mere lip service if they did not have sincere feelings and actions to secure the well being for other people.

My sincere answer is that I do not want to become a politician. I only wish to follow my father's behest and become a good physician because I really think, "A good physician is a loving mother."

I now have a path, a direction for my activities. If by any chance they bear any fruit financially, I will happily donate it to:

- Reconstruct my country, Vietnam.
- Help children and people in other poor countries build and rebuild their schools, factories, and businesses.

Our actions should be directed toward the Good, and humanitarianism should be the final aim of our life.

Now I would like to use al the knowledge that I have learned to sincerely contribute to the welfare of humankind.

As we all know, each individual among us is a micro-universe in the macro-universe. We are like the flowers, leaves and fruit in the universe-tree. As human beings, we are all brothers and sisters sharing the same home and the same Mother Earth. We all share the similarity in anatomy and in the nervous system except for the differences in gender or states of health.

We have a lot of things to study about the universe and man. In this book, I would like to focus mainly on 7 basic vital points in our body and a number of interesting facts in the cultures of Asia, Europe, and America for our application. These items have been carefully chosen to serve as basic information and clear yardstick instrumental to the search of balance for the current as well as for future generations. But I also need your indispensable assistance to form a union to make our common universe-tree brighter so that our posterity can enjoy peace and happiness.

I. BACK TO YOUR OWN HEART:

"It exists before Heaven and Earth
Quiet and amorphous
Capable of lording it over all living beings and things
And undisturbed by the four seasons."

Lao Tse

Just reading these words is enough to leave us in awe. "What in the world has such power that it is not swayed by the four seasons?" It is our true Heart. Being true means calm, unperturbed through time and space. It is the light of our Heart in every one of us.

We all have to struggle for life. Sometimes because of the chaotic situation in each society or country, True Heart may be alienated. Now if we want to build something stable, we have to re-find our True Heart. Only True Heart can redeem us and reconcile us in a true and everlasting love.

In the twenty-first century, scientific and technological progress has attained a very high level, providing mankind with all sorts of material convenience. But at the same time, it is also bringing us to the verge of self-destruction. If we wish to have a perfect life and a fair chance of survival, we must start with a truly ethical foundation built by our own hands. Only then can a paradise on Earth be materialized.

To bring True Heart back to us, we need to take the Qi (vital energy) from the fire of kidney upward. To make this process clearer, let us begin with one important point in our body, the point of Yong Quan (Kid 1).

"Yong" means "powerful"
"Quan" means "stream" or "spring"
"Yong Quan" means "powerful stream"

To achieve any goal, we ought to have a strong will nourished by the Fire of our kidney. If we want to march steadily with peace and happiness into the twenty-first century, we must rely on a source of strength in our body. This source is the point of Yong Quan. It is the starting point of the Lesser Yin-Kidney Channel of Foot.

<u>Position:</u> The point of Yong Quan is located on the sole of the foot at 1/3 of the distance from the base of the second toe to the heel.

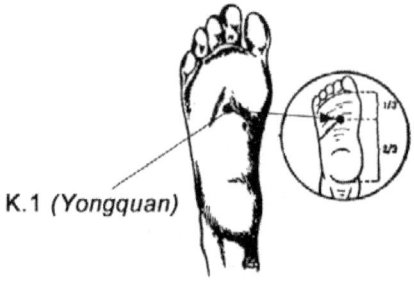

K.1 *(Yongquan)*

<u>Traditional functions:</u> It opens the sense in the mouth and calms the mind.

<u>Traditional indications:</u> The opening of this point can cure dizziness, headache in the crown, blurred vision, swollen throat, high blood pressure, hysteria, infantile convulsion, paralysis in the leg, insomnia, edema, stroke, nosebleed, difficult urination, diarrhea, colic, insanity, hot soles of feet, pain in tiptoe.

(Acupuncture - A Comprehensive Text - Shanghai College of Traditional Medicine translated and edited by John O'Connor and Dan Bensky)

II. DIFFERENCE BETWEEN LIFE AND THE TAO (Religion):

"The Tao exists right in this world
And cannot be understood anywhere else
Looking for Enlightenment elsewhere
Means you seek a rabbit with horns."

Founding Monk Hue Nang

Everything from human beings to all other species is the offspring of Mother Earth. From the creation of the earth until now, we have been learning a lot of lessons about the Good and the Evil.

The preceding poem teaches us that Buddhism and human ethics are closely related to this world. We cannot get away from life to seek its truth or enlightenment. Trying to find ethics but losing touch with life is something like trying to find a rabbit with horns. We will never find such a rabbit just as we will never find true happiness. A rabbit with horns is a thing that will never occur in life.

So, are there any possible relationships between life and the Tao? Life means our everyday activities, our struggle to survive.

The Tao has 2 meanings:

(a) The way
(b) Separation from worldly life to practice religion for one's own good by following the steps of the Buddha, Jesus Christ, or other saints. The "Tao" also means an assembly of people studying religious philosophies to seek truth for life and try to achieve "The True, the Good and the Beautiful."

The Tao can also be known as the world's cultures that help people know where they came from and how they can survive on Earth.

All of us want to follow a noble way regardless of whatever religion they practice achieving a good and everlasting life. In everyday activities, the sense of reason is present in our subconscious and as a result we are able to distinguish between right and wrong.

In my childhood, when I did something wrong, I was quite aware of it. We all have the ability to tell what is right or wrong, good, or evil, in light or in darkness.

Life is also for the sake of art. Everybody longs for a beautiful existence just as a plant always turns toward sunlight if it is to grow fully.

Religious goals are the same: to improve oneself, to ennoble one's mentality and to get rid of sufferings. On a broader scale, religion seeks to build a better society and guide people from ignorance to the bright realm of the True, the Good and the Beautiful and in perfect harmony with Heaven and Earth.

Therefore, we can say that life and the Tao (religion) share more similarities than differences. They both aim at building a better life and a brighter future for mankind.

After having faced a lot of hardships and sufferings, a good foundation for our society tends to become less stable. The worry of drifting away from one's origin and fear for one's survival seem to be rampant in everybody's mind. At the beginning of the twenty-first century, the anxiety about the future of the young generations and of our children was bearing down heavily on every family and on the shoulders of any learned man.

Today we should apply this lesson of Vo Tuong (No Form) to our life. Establish a practical social ethics for the development of our own selves, of all people and of our country. Only then will we feel no fear for our survival. We should master our fear and we will be able to work for the creation of everlasting happiness and peace for us and for future generations. Paradise is within our reach provided we unite our minds and our hearts.

The key to survival lies in our own hands. Whether it goes up or down, prospers or falls apart, the fate of this world will entirely depend upon all of us.

This key to survival can be started with the Fire of Ming Men in every one of us. It is the gate that helps light the vital lamp. Only by controlling and utilizing this lamp can we realize our wish as described in this phrase: "Glory to God in the highest sky. Peace on Earth to men of good will."

A Good Heart is the light dormant within every one of us from the dawn of human history. We should return to it in order to re-establish everlasting peace. To find this vital light we need the fire of the Governing Channel and Yang Channel located in our back. It is the fire of Yin and Yang kidneys, the door to our survival. To give more information on this, I would like to show the need to open a vital point in our body, the point of Ming Men (Du 4).

The point of Ming Men (Du. 4):

Ming Men is defined as "Life's Door". We all know that life begins with birth. Ming Men is the Living Fire of our body. When the fire is on, we live. When the fire goes out, we die.

Location: Ming Men point is located in the middle of the spinal column between the 2nd and 3rd lumbar vertebrae.

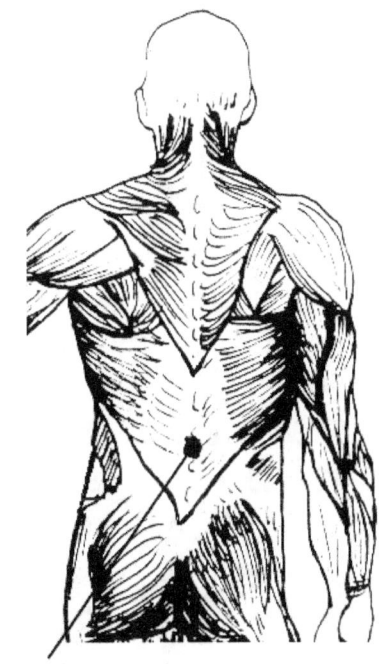

DU.4 *(Mingmen)*

Traditional functions: Once this point is opened, it will help us nourish the source of our Qi, strengthen our 2 kidneys and at the same time consolidate our backbone.

Traditional Indications: The opening of this point will cure backache, calcification of the backbone, impotence, and the following illnesses:

- Early ejaculation, leukorrhea, enteritis, nephritis, sciatica, low back pain, infantile paralysis, headache, infantile convulsion, spermatorrhea, hemorrhage in the urinary tract, serious constipation, pain of intestinal colic and enuresis.

(Acupuncture - A Comprehensive Text - Shanghai College of Traditional Medicine translated and edited by John O'Connor and Dan Bensky)

III. BENEVOLENCE:

Fate has brought us together so that we can join our hands in an interrupted circle to help build a better world for generations to come. If you share this goal with me, I would like to take you on a tour to acquaint us with the cultures of the three continents:

Asia – Europe - America

Throughout man's history we have been given a rich legacy of cultures by many races. But in this book, I will touch on only a small part of it. The part that I think we can apply to our plan of actions. Nothing will be better or more beautiful than collecting and sharing the essence of the world's cultures for our joint undertaking.

We all know that we get nutritious honey from a beehive. Its workers fly tin all directions gathering pure nectar to make honey for their hive. And speaking of the beehive, if we take a little moment to observe it, we can see that no structures can be compared with it for its order and neatness. We can learn from a beehive just as we can learn from the world's cultures. The bees make honey for their posterity just like our ancestors leaving their cultures for us. So, I hope we all can enjoy cultures as we do with honey.

We can also show our gratitude to Mother Earth by promoting and sharing the good things from these cultures.

I wish that we would use knowledge gained from these cultures to build an organized and stable society so that future generations can share the result of this work in harmony and with an ascendant spirit. Nothing is more beautiful than the harmony between various cultures of different generations. It will help build a beautiful and lasting life for all of us.

1. ASIAN CULTURE:

a. Living with a Kind heart:

- Vietnamese Culture:

Our country, originally called Van Lang is a small nation to the south of China. Its history has seen innumerable sufferings and upheavals since the founding days. But we have survived all the changes because we have a very simple and sincere character taught and handed down by our ancestors to develop our heart and body, "Living with a Kind Heart."

To be able to live with a Kind Heart, we should know how to distinguish right from wrong, to judge things with wisdom, to deal with one another fairly. In family, community, or society, we should respect our elders and be tolerant to our juniors.

To keep living with a Kind Heart is to pursue the good and avoid the evil. It also is our constant effort to improve ourselves physically and spiritually and set a good example to others around us.

This moral guidance is so simple, so gentle and yet it has been entrenched deeply in Vietnamese mentality and handed down from generation to generation.

Vietnam has experienced uncountable ups and downs in its long history: wars, foreign occupations, colonial rules, and exoduses of its people to all Four Corners of the world. But no matter where we live, no matter how hard life is, we never forget this sacred teaching by our ancestors.

We use it as our foundation, our compass for survival and for keeping balance to accommodate ourselves to any living conditions.

In today's life, fierce competition emerges in the dominant mode of human survival. All of us know that everybody needs to earn his bread to support himself and his family. In every walk of life, in every field of business or profession, the phrase "life is a struggle" still remains true. As this struggle gets harder and harder, its consequence gets worse and worse. Dishonesty, cheating and making profits at other people's expense become prevailing.

We have seen many of these instances. But if we just stand by idly, what will be the future of our children and ourselves?

The challenge of this hellish way of existence does indeed scare us when we think of our own fate and that of our posterity. Our fear arises from the fact that what we lack most is not material things but humaneness. We feel extremely lonely and helpless because we do not see beautiful ideals in life anymore. Our young generations are not receiving any firm support from their elders and are in danger of becoming astray and corrupt. The sense of ascension is not cherished any more. From this moral decline, many gangs are formed and are causing trouble everywhere.

In their lifetime, a lot of saints and sages had warned us of these evils, but we did not pay attention. Without moral foundation, wealth and material frivolities provided by advanced science and technology have blinded us wickedly. This imbalance is really so prevalent that our present life is seriously harmed.

Dear readers, I wholeheartedly invite you to contribute your knowledge and efforts in restoring the natural balance for a beautiful existence for our coming generations and ourselves. I earnestly wish that our dream would soon be realized. So, let us join our hands to light up the Bright Universal Lamp and dispel the Evil Darkness that has blackened our life. This darkness is nothing but craftiness, deception and depravity that are taking away noble ideas about life and pushing us to the brink of the abyss of loneliness.

To light up this pure and magnanimous lamp, all of us must keep ourselves balanced. Once thus done, we have lit up our own lamps. Lamps and fuel essential to the lighting were bestowed to us from our birth. This fuel takes its source from the heart and gets burnt into flame by the Fire of the Kidneys. We ought to create for ourselves good will and open our hearts and minds so that the Fire of Kidneys can burn brightly. When our lamps have been lit, we have to join, unite and share... Only then can our Great Universal Lamp succeed in growing and illuminating far and near.

When we plant crops, we choose the best seeds. We take good cares of them by fertilizing and watering them every day. Similarly, we repeat this process when we want to develop good concepts for our life.

b. "Each person should attain a complete individual balance: absorb the neutral power between Yin and Yang and consequently achieve bliss on Earth." Angeline Lan Doan, O.M.D.

We all are children of Mother Earth. Each person has his own character, his own soul, and his own human electricity. Humankind is the most intelligent and balanced species. We stand with heads toward Heaven to assimilate Yang Qi and feet on Earth to get Yin Qi.

HEAVEN – MAN - EARTH

Man is the link between Heaven and Earth. His survival is possible thanks to a number of favorable factors: food from animal and plant sources, minerals, and vitamins.

Whether we follow oriental or western medicine, our body is made up of water, matter and human electricity from Yin and Yang.

A healthy person depends on a lot of factors:

- Spirit (consisting of learning and self-improvement as mentioned above)
- Body with its internal organs, its nervous system, and its excretory system in good working conditions.
- Thoughts that must be aimed at the Good just as our head always turns toward the light.

Whoever has a healthy body, and a clear mind must be considered very blessed because other people may inherit some diseases from their parents, which forms a family, a society, or a nation.

All of us live in a certain environment. As a member of these groupings, we have to observe their rules and laws. When our heart is calm, stable, and not disturbed by these obligations, we will feel happy, peaceful, and blessed. On the contrary, if our heart is perturbed, our body controlled by external conditions, we cannot find any happiness on Earth even if we sit on a pile of gold.

Therefore, paradise or hell is something felt in our heart. Outward materials are only additional ornaments. These materials can be compared to a layer of paint to enhance beauty. But real beauty ought not to be on the outside only; it must be on the inside, too.

The important thing is a not a magnificent external trapping but a healthy body and a happy mind.

Naturally, an average person among us will choose a happy life with a full stomach and a calm mind, which he should strive to get for himself.

To achieve these things, we should follow this Oriental medicine principle, "In Yin there is Yang and in Yang there is Yin." Everything in this world originates from the combination of Yin and Yang. Attaining the balance between these two crucial factors will make us stable and healthy physically and spiritually.

In nature, all things interact and are divided into Yin and Yang like black and white, male, and female. This is a natural law that controls everything present even before the creation of our world. We may use different terms to describe things, but their characteristics stay the same.

Man is Yang

Woman is Yin

Right leg and arm are Yang

Left leg and arm are Yin

Bacteria are divided into Yin and Yang

Human spermatozoa are also divided into Yin and Yang.

A heart has left and right auricles for oxygen poor and oxygen-enriched blood. Oxygen-poor blood is considered as black and hence Yin. Oxygen-enriched blood is considered as red and hence Yang. Liver, lung, and kidney are also divided in Yin and Yang.

All species have males and females. Foods and minerals taken from earth also have Yin matter and Yang matter.

A political system of a nation is also based on the principle of Yin and Yang. In the United States, the Republican Party can be called Yang and the Democratic Party Yin. In the world, communists are Yin and capitalists are Yang.

To put it more clearly, we are now faced with Yin and Yang in many shapes. In whatever situation, if Yin and Yang are balanced, we can attain the spirit of happiness and enlightenment. Lingshu-Benshenpian once said, "The origin of life is in the Life Essence (the male and female semen). When these two unite to make one, it is called the spirit."

When the two powers of Yin and Yang are balanced by a neutral power, they are not in control. Then we have found our True Heart.

When we attain a calm vacuum, we have found balance (our own neutral power). This is the time when we have found happiness and paradise on the highest level of the calm vacuum.

Neutrality is without Yin or Yang, with "matter" and also without "matter." This is the state of supreme goodness, beauty, and peacefulness when we can distinguish between Yin and Yang, between right and wrong without any impartiality.

This supreme neutrality without form originates from our True Heart, our "original identity." It existed before the creation and is inherent in every one of us. Let us read these words, "The Heart houses the Spirit, the Lungs the Animal Soul, the Liver the Spiritual Soul, the Spleen the Mind and the Kidneys the Will." (Su Wen Xuanming Wugi Lun).

In short, if we want to achieve happiness with a calm heart, we need to train ourselves with good ideas and actions. Our heart plays a very crucial role because it helps circulate blood; (oxygen-poor and oxygen-enriched) which is the source of life for our internal organs. Our brain needs blood to work and all other systems in our body need it to function properly.

When we have gained the neutral power (calm vacuum), our heart feels happy and blessed without being influenced by the outside world. When our heart is happy, we then will be able to share this good feeling with other people and ennoble our life.

The heart is a micro-universe, but its feelings can be as large as a macro-universe. It can develop and engross all corners of the globe to help mankind light up the universal lamp.

Therefore, we can build ourselves a paradise on Earth with all the available materials. The key to this paradise lies in our Heart. Each one of us has his own ways to open the Heart. The important thing is that we need time and perseverance to realize what our Heart sincerely wishes for.

The sun from Father Heaven is shining to welcome all of us to be reunited under the same roof of Mother Earth. Let us rejoice at our bright future!

"From far and near in the world
Yin and Yang form a perfect combination.
Our life is full of "Being" and "Not Being"
Only Mind-Heart Harmony can bring about happiness."

To have this supreme neutral power (calm vacuum of the Heart) we have to muster energy from the Leg Greater Yang Small Bladder Channel. This sea of energy is the point Tianzhu and the neutral power is the point Shanzhong of the Conception Channel and Yin Channel of the body.

The point of Tianzhu (UB.10): Tianzhu means "Heaven's Pillar." It is considered as a pillar of our body. It helps us keep balance and stand erect. Just like houses need strong pillars to stand firmly, nations and the world need talented people to develop.

Location: Tianzhu is about 1.3 units lateral to Yamen Point (GV.15) on the back of the neck.

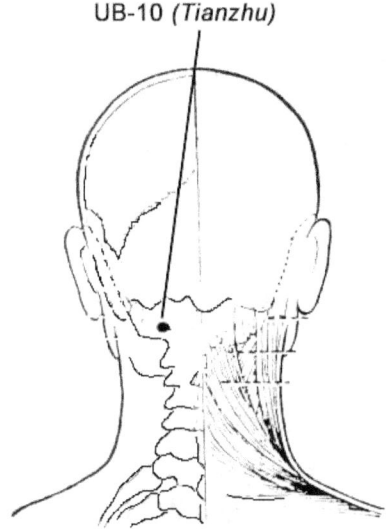

UB-10 *(Tianzhu)*

- Yamen point (GV.15): Yamen means "Door of Muteness"

Location: About 0.5 units above the natural hairline on the nape of the neck, between the spinous processes of the 1st and 2nd cervical vertebrae.

Traditional Indications: Opening of this point can help laryngitis, eye diseases, and infantile convulsions penetrating odor." It cures these illnesses: headache, dizziness, and nasal congestion.

GV.15 *(Yamen)*

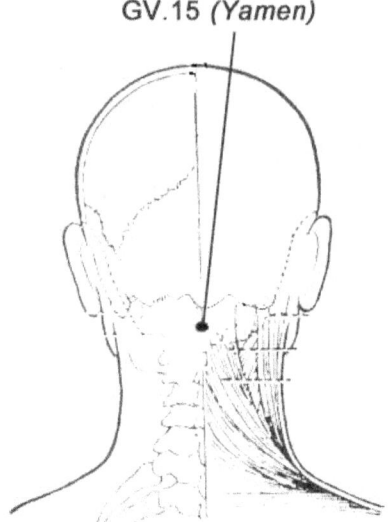

- The point of Shanzhong (CV.17): This promotes sharpness and excellence of the balance between the point that belongs to the Yin Channel. Shanzhong means "Yin and Yang in our body. Everything needs a perfect balance of these two principles to last long.

Location: On the sternum, level with the nipples of the breasts, or between and just above the articulations of the right and left fifth rib with sternum.

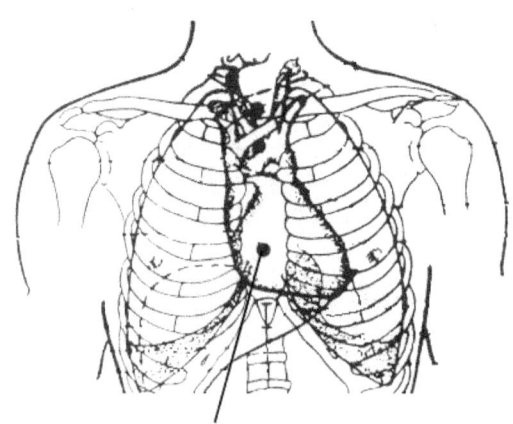

REN. 17 *(Shanzhong)*

Traditional indications: Opening of this point can cure wheezing, panting, spitting and coughing blood, difficulty or inability to swallow food (due to constriction or dryness in the esophagus), tumors on the neck, lung abscess, chest pain.

We can reach the goal of "The True, The Good and The Beautiful" if we succeed in achieving the union of Yin and Yang. This means that when our Heart, which is Yin and our body, which is Yang, unites in a common ideal, our Heart and body will attain peace and happiness. In other words when Yin and Yang in our body unite, we will enjoy happiness. When they separate, we will experience suffering. Our body is a synthesis of Yin and Yang, a tangible thing created by God.

Example 1:

In a human body, the back is Yang, and the chest is Yin. The internal organs are also divided into Yin and Yang. When our body is healthy and our mind is clear, our thoughts are aimed at noble and beautiful ideals, undisturbed by the outside world. Then our Yin and Yang are in perfect union.

Example 2:

In family life, wife and husband are an instance of the union between Yin and Yang. If the spouses are in agreement or cherish the same ideal, they can achieve happiness. But if they don't share the same ideal, have different characters or one of them is not interested in improving his or her morals, their family will soon be broken up or at least left in disarray. The situation will become worse if Yin and Yang are in conflict. There is no balance, no happiness but only hell.

On a broader scale, we have to apply the same spirit to build a foundation for a better society, better nations, or a better world. A paradise can only be established when we succeed in bringing about a perfect union between spirit (Yin) and matter (Yang) and then we can enjoy happiness together.

"The Sandalwood fragrance is wafting from afar,
Coming from Heaven's well of jade.
Realizing the Yin and Yang balance,
With unity we can achieve the Good and the Beautiful."

For each individual's life, each family or each country, a clear goal and a direction for actions must be set up. To do so, we first have to pose ourselves these questions: What does each of us want? What is our goal? What will be our future? Then we need to ensure that thoughts and actions must be clearly in unison. Moreover, we should ensure that the benefits of our actions are not only for ourselves but also for everybody. We should always ask ourselves if our actions are right and if other people around us are able to share our happiness.

For the purposes just mentioned, I would like to contribute my small part from my own experience and the knowledge I have gathered throughout my own life. So far, they have helped me find the direction for actions and enjoy happiness in my heart and in my family.

c. Ten important concepts of the term "HIGHEST" The path of Ascension (Toward Yang or Aiming at the Good):

- Highest God
- Highest Direction
- Highest Man
- Highest Light
- Highest Heart
- Highest Earth
- Highest Door
- Highest Mouth
- Highest Neutrality & Loyalty
- Highest Happiness

All the theories or teachings left behind by mankind's saints from olden times are only means for us to direct our actions. The important thing is our goal, our destination. Just as in a voyage when we reach our destination, we do not need the vehicle anymore. What matters to us is whether these theories are helpful to our present life or not.

Now, I would like to recall a turning point in Vietnam's history when many of us were scampering everywhere for a boat to go abroad to find a new life. When we were on board, we then thought of some food to soothe our hunger.

After that we wished we could reach a free country soon. But when we arrived in another country, we were once again overwhelmed with lots of other wishes and yearnings as well as questions about our new life. Each of us had different thoughts and different wishes. The boats that some of us took to cross the sea are now only memories of the past. We are now faced with problems that require directions for our new life.

I am compiling here ten important concepts of the term "Highest" because we now need vehicles to carry us to our goals. These concepts will also give us directions for our path. The starting guideline is: "The forefinger points at the Moon. This Moon is nothing but our own Heart."

Beginning with our own heart and mind is not a political path but a pure yardstick from the "Bright light of the Sun and the Moon." What does this mean? Our brain is the light from the Sun. Our heart is the love from the Moon.

The Sun symbolizes our brain that always learns, trains, and creates.

The Moon symbolizes our heart that always purifies our feelings.

Our heart and our brain have to coordinate so that our body functions properly and forms a good shelter for our soul. Our sacred soul can be considered a precious jewel bestowed us by Heaven. This bright light of the sun and the moon is the innate Qi (Energy), which is our soul. It can burn forever if we know how to preserve it.

I now need it, and my dear readers, you do too. This is the way to bring you longevity that I am going to explain to you step by step.

i. Highest God:

Heaven or God is a great symbol to us. We have not seen Heaven or God, but when we speak of Heaven, we usually refer to it as God, the Almighty Being who determines everything for all species. Then, who is Heaven or God? To understand more about ancient people's thoughts and beliefs consecrated to the Almighty God, we should go over history books and the history of various countries in the world.

The universe is immense and limitless. Our earth is like a microcosm in a macrocosm. It is one planet of the solar system. This system consists of 9 planets that orbit around the sun. They are:

- Jupiter
- Mercury
- Saturn
- Neptune
- Mars
- Venus
- Uranus
- Pluto
- Earth

There are myriads of galaxies located far away from ours. Some of them we have found, but many of them we have not because of their distant positions. It takes millions and millions of light years to reach them (The speed of light is about 186,000 miles per second). Now let us return to our earth. Our planet and our moon get their light from the sun. It brightens everything. This light is our soul and the pure spirit of nature. For this reason, people in ancient Egypt believed that the sun is the Almighty God, and they worshipped the sun.

In ancient literature, we have many examples of praises to the sun, "Sun God: Thou art beautiful, mighty, bright shining and supreme in every land and thy beams enfold the earth to the very limits of thy creation..." (14th Astronomer Royal - The Sun)

The sun is glorified as the lamp of the earth, the hope for survival. It is the symbol for a happy with the True, the Good and the Beautiful that mankind is aiming at.

From the Fable of Acis, Drygen 1631-1700, "The glorious lamp of Heaven, the radiant Sun is Nature's eyes."

But here, we should know that God is in every person. Every one of us is a little and separate cosmos, but it is combined with others to form a big universe.

The sun is our father who has given us life on our planet. Then Mother Earth nourishes us. The sun is not only for mankind. All living organisms depend on Father Sun and Mother Earth to survive. We cannot see the face of this Supreme God, but He sees our actions and us clearly.

In Ancient Egypt, the rising of the sun in the east is compared to the beginning of life, "O living after, beginning of life! When you arise on the eastern horizon, you fill every land with your beauty." (From Joseph Kaster's the Literature and Myth of Ancient Egypt.)

Therefore, the Almighty God has given us life and He is present in our body and soul. He is present in everybody and everything in nature. We can say that everybody or everything is a little embodiment of the Almighty God.

The Supreme God has given us life and resides in our spirit and in our heart. All human beings and other species are examples of his microcosms.

In Hindu literature we find this praise, "Adore the sun, rising with all his rays, receiving the obeisance of Gods and demons, the shining maker of light." (The Epic Hindu poem Ramayana, 300 B. C.)

We can see clearly that His face is as bright as sunlight, and He is present in ourselves in the form of every present radiant solar ray. As His little embodiment, we are learning to improve ourselves in order to achieve our own enlightenment.

As a conclusion, we can say that the Almighty God is in each one of us. With this realization in mind, we should always treat one another with respect and equality. Our Almighty God has created a grandiose universe, but his favorite creation must be mankind. The Almighty God, our Father Heaven has endowed His humans with the most precious gifts, the Earth, and the support from the Sun God.

For her part, Mother Earth has been nourishing us with great love. We should act as good sons in such a way to deserve her love. To do this, we have to protect, respect Mother Earth, and reciprocate her caring concern for us with love and support not only for her but also for all of us.

How sad will Mother Earth be if this land is polluted or destroyed by her own children? And this pollution and destruction will kill them by their own senseless acts. We all have to try our best to save our Mother Earth. Do not let contamination, rotting or diseases spread everywhere. To reciprocate her care for us, we must unite our minds and hearts to safeguard our environment, our beloved Mother. How good it is if we can do this!

Mother Earth will be saved, and she will not grieve any more because her children know how and what to do to adore Father Heaven and Mother Earth.

"O Great God!
You have come to us.
What a sacred meeting it is!
O Father, Mother and Children
How tender your love is!
Father, Mother and Children
How happy it is!
Heaven, Earth, and Humans are bound.
How immense and loving it is!
The sacred torch is lit brightly.
Vibrant with new vital energy.
O Great God!"

ii. Highest Man:

Among all species, humans are the most balanced and intelligent, but also the weakest. An average person can hardly carry 100 pounds and climb upward. But an ant can carry something twice its weight and go up a wall. Pound for pound, this tiny insect is stronger than a human.

Speaking of breathing, we can only hold our breath for about 1 to 3 minutes, but other animals can do this longer than we do.

In this part, I would like to say only about humans' good things. Although their bodies are weak, their intelligence has helped them invent or construct great contraptions or architectures such as the world's seven wonders. Today the development of computers has taken mankind almost to the peak of civilization. Thanks to science and technology brought about by human intelligence, we can live in a wonderful magic-like world. Through many upheavals and changes, mankind still survives because the power of their brain has helped them unite and create.

We need many factors to form a good person. It is the same with the world. A combination of the best parts in the culture and civilization of every race, in every country is necessary for us to make this planet a better place to live.

Human intelligence has enabled many successes in science. One of these is a computer, which are now rapidly changing the face of our world. These successes have made our life more civilized. But we cannot deny the fact that there are still a number of negative aspects arising from scientific and technological progress.

In this part of the "Highest Man", I would like to emphasize human superiority over other species. I wish to share and contribute my part to weave an immense web of culture and science in the direction of the True, the Good and the Beautiful.

To achieve a balance between Heaven-Earth-Human, we need a juncture between the "old" and the "new" order, from Yin to Yang or from the "dark" to the "bright". From the knowledge of mankind, we learn that this juncture is the generous and calm heart and the powerful mind needed to accomplish the Heaven-Earth-Humans harmony.

In this new century, we have to unite our hearts and minds to attain the golden principles of the True, the Good and the Beautiful.

What does "Highest Man" really mean? It means that we have to combine our happy hearts and our creative intelligence to serve ourselves, other people, and the human race. We should always learn to promote "the good" and reduce "the bad". Leaders of a group, a country or the whole world ought to provide optimal conditions to facilitate the balanced advancement of these communities.

> *"There are Humans in Heaven,*
> *Earth in Humans*
> *And Heaven in Earth."*

When humans are in equal and harmonious relations, they deserve the term "Highest Man".

> *"Man is the highest under Heaven,*
> *Always trying to gain Peace and Happiness.*
> *We need to cherish liberty,*
> *Cause it is a gift from Heaven.*
> *We need to practice Benevolence*
> *And offer it as a jewel to Father Heaven."*

iii. Highest Heart:

In every animal's body, the heart is the most important organ. It is like the nucleus of an atom. It is needed for the circulation of blood to keep an animal alive.

The heart is also said to be the house for feelings and emotions in humans and other animals.

We can now mention some thoughts about the heart in a number of Oriental medical books.

"The Heart houses the Spirit. The Lungs the Animal Soul, the Liver the Spiritual Soul, the Spleen the Mind and the Kidneys the Will." (Su Wen, Xuan Ming Wugi Lun)

In the book "Medical Principles of Hai Thuong" (by Lan Ong Le Huu Trac), the heart is regarded as the master of the body. It contains the spirit, which is one of the three human treasures (essence, energy, and spirit).

Essence refers to bone, marrow, essential fluids, and blood. Energy is the life force. Spirit encompasses all aspects of the mind or soul. Spirit is considered an invisible part of human beings.

The heart controls the spirit and belongs to the Trigram "Li", corresponding to the south. The Kidneys belong to the Trigram "K'an" and corresponding to the North. The human senses of seeing and hearing depend on the heart and the kidneys. Also, in "Nei Jing" (Chinese "Canon of Medicine") we have this observation, "When the controlling is not correct, the organs will suffer." It means that if the heart does not control well, the viscera will be in trouble. Or "when the heart is sick the spirit will perish." It means that if the heart does not propel blood to the brain, the latter will be in serious danger. Therefore, the heart is the master of the body, the pillar of the viscera and the nervous system.

Su Wen also said about Yin and Yang in the human body. "When speaking of Yin and Yang, the exterior is Yang, the interior is Yin. When speaking of Yin and Yang in the human body, the back is Yang, the abdomen Yin. When speaking of Yin and Yang of the Zang and Fu in the body, then the Zang are Yin, the Fu are Yang. Liver, Heart, Spleen, Lungs and Kidneys are all Yin. The Gall Bladder, Stomach, Large Intestine, Small Intestine, Bladder and Triple Warmer are all Yang.

Thus, the back is Yang and the Yang within the Yang is the heart.

The back is Yang, and the Yin within the Yang is the lungs.

The abdomen is Yin, and the Yin within the Yin is the kidneys

The abdomen is Yin, and the Yang within the Yin is the liver.

The abdomen is Yin, and the extreme Yin within the Yin is the Spleen" (Su Wen, Jin Kui Zhenyan Lun)

When we speak of Yin and Yang, we speak of the balance between the two poles: positive and negative. In the human body, the heart and the kidney support each other. Thus, Yin and Yang interact.

The heart belongs to Trigram "Li", being hollow inside and Yin goes down. The kidneys belong to the Trigram "K'an", being full inside and Yang goes up (Here once more we see the interaction: in Yin there is Yang; in Yang there is Yin). Besides the kidneys' assistance, the heart is divided into left and right auricles propelling oxygen-poor and oxygen-enriched blood through the body.

The heart is considered the house of the spirit. So, we need to have a sound spirit to keep the heart healthy. Each of us has to decide and choose a noble path to follow and to bear responsibility for our actions.

The heart is also divided into positive and negative. Oxygen-enriched blood is positive. This also means good health, Noble Energy and bright light. Oxygen-poor blood is negative. This denotes sickness, poor energy, and baseness.

Our choice depends on many factors. The most important ones are determination and self-control of our heart. When our heart is calm and determined, we can distinguish between good and evil, right, and wrong clearly.

In reality, clearness is always glorified just as oxygen-rich blood nourishes the body and its organs. Clearness of our mind is like the light that dispels darkness. When bright light is achieved, we can do good things and help others. Therefore, each person should gain light to brighten him or her and the positive goal must be our direction in life.

Nature is very helpful to life and every one of us longs for longevity.

The sage Quan Thanh Tu once said, "If you want to achieve longevity, do not overwork your body and do not disturb your mind."

We should follow the right way of macrobiotics to nature true energy. The ancient sages used to live in calmness and tranquility. They always chose to do work that was beneficial to themselves and others. They never did anything that was harmful to their life. Therefore, they were able to enjoy a long life.

"When the spirit is calm, life is long.

When the spirit is lost, the body is damaged."

That is why we have to nourish our spirit carefully.

When dealing with other people, we ought to treat them with feelings that come from our true heart such as care, equality, and benevolence. We should always try to share and support one another. We need to follow the principle "There is Yang in Yin and Yin in Yang" if we want to achieve a balance that can help us live a long life. When we apply this principle to our actions, we fully understand the wonderful meaning of the "Highest Heart". Lao Tse once said, "People who never show off their high virtues are indeed highly virtuous."

To conclude, we can say that the heart is not only important to our body but also to our spirit because it helps us choose the right path for ourselves.

> *"Everything begins with the heart.*
> *It helps achieve concord,*
> *And equality among us.*
> *We can distinguish between right and wrong.*
> *Thanks to the Highest Heart.*
> *It lights a lamp in our mind*
> *To reach the goals of the Good and the Beautiful."*

iv. Highest Door:

A door is an entrance to a place such as a house, a cave, or a building. How can we get through the door to enter a place? We need a key to open it.

In order to have the right key to open the door, we need to follow the Yin -Yang principle. If we can achieve the balance between Yin and Yang, our body will not be attacked by external causes of illness. If we have a healthy body and a good immune system, no outside factors can enter the door of our body to make us sick.

The spirit is considered the door of our body. Our heart is the key to open it to welcome sincere love, share good things and promote progress of sciences.

We need to have a large door full of generosity and humanness balanced with the principle of Yin and Yang to lead us to happiness and high virtues for all of mankind.

This door also guides us to a bright future for our future generations. This is also the door to a sun-lit spring day bringing with it promises of a better and safer world for all species.

This door opens to advanced technology and high civilizations, which help bring about peace and happiness to mankind.

Our heart will also need to know when to close the door to protect our body when we see anything that may harm us.

I think that you, my dear readers, will agree with me and try to establish such a good door for us.

"The spring wind is blowing through the door
Making my mind dreaming
And my heart deeply moved.
My thin body is full of vitality.
My heart is open
To smile and welcome spring
In the sun-lit pine forest.
How beautiful life is!"

v. Highest Neutrality and Loyalty:

Among the factors that represent the activities of the two poles Yin and Yang, there are five counteracting elements: Wood, Fire, and Earth, Metal and Water. When they are in perfect balance, our body is free of illnesses.

Su Wen said, "The five elements: Wood, Fire, Earth, Metal and Water encompass all the phenomena of nature. It is a symbolism that applies itself equal to man."

When there is neutralization between the 2 poles Yin and Yang, humans will have a healthy body and balanced mind. The old medical book "Nei Jing" said, "When Yin and Yang are in harmony, our spirit is balanced."

Notes:

Water is Yin
Fire is Yang
Wood = Liver, Gall bladder
Fire = Heart, Small Intestine
Earth = Spleen and Stomach
Metal = Lung, Large Intestine
Water = Kidney, Bladder

THE FIVE ELEMENTS

Gall Bladder [+]
Liver [-]
WOOD

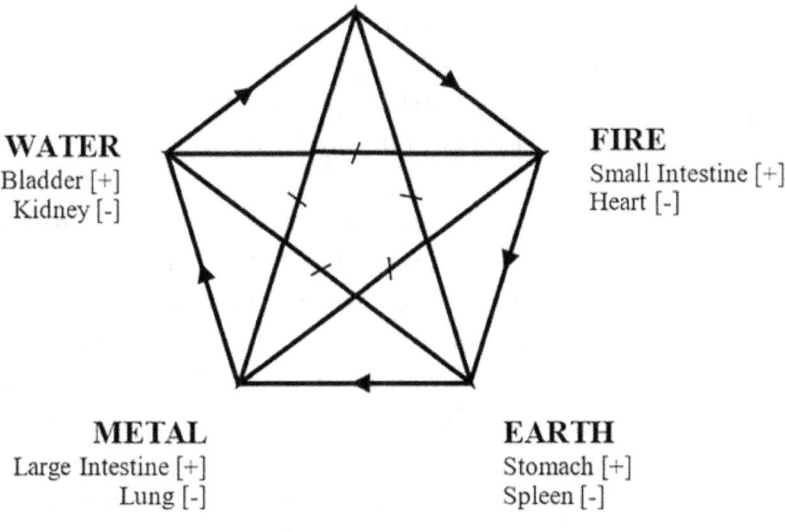

WATER
Bladder [+]
Kidney [-]

FIRE
Small Intestine [+]
Heart [-]

METAL
Large Intestine [+]
Lung [-]

EARTH
Stomach [+]
Spleen [-]

→ **Generating Sequences**

—╱— **Over-acting Sequences**

Neutrality and equality are necessary for humans' relations among themselves and with other species in nature.

Harmony is an art in life. In a musical piece, the sounds and words must be in good harmony to make it a great musical work. In a painting, colors and background must be in harmony to make it a masterpiece. In nature, there must also be balance. If there is no balance, there may be disasters.

In one word, everything from little to big must have balance to make it work properly. Otherwise, there may be serious trouble or even destruction. In our relations, loyalty is a necessary character not only among humans but also among other species. When we grow any plants and take care of them, there is an attachment between them and us. When we raise an animal, take good care of it and live close to it, we see its loyal feelings toward us. These are the good fruits brought about by our good acts.

Nature has taught us many valuable lessons such as if we want to have a good harvest, we need to take good care of our crops. Therefore, we must try our best to develop our balance and loyalty so that we can take good care of our life and nature.

In order to do this; our heart and our spirit need to be also in balance. Lack of this harmony will lead us to death (Old Literature).

According to the Book of Change (I-Ching), from "Emptiness" comes "the Supreme Ultimate". When the "Supreme Ultimate" moves, Yang is born. When the "Supreme Ultimate" rests, Yin is born. In human breathing, inhalation and exhalation are phases of Yin and Yang. Changes in nature are also expressions of Yin and Yang.

During the creation, Yin and Yang's merging and interaction created all living organisms. Yin and Yang although formless are the basis of life. Water and fire, hot and cold are also phases of Yin and Yang.

From Yin and Yang harmony, we have life. When there is balance between Yin and Yang, we are physically and spiritually healthy. Therefore, we have to learn from nature and try our best to achieve balance not only for our body but also for the relations between human beings.

When our life is in perfect balance, we will enjoy happiness and serenity in our heart and spirit.

> *"Heaven has determined*
> *The balance between Yin and Yang,*
> *To bring us happiness.*
> *Our heart is full of blood*
> *To propel our love for life*
> *And achieve peace and balance*
> *According to nature's law."*

vi. Highest Direction:

Everything comes from a source, a tiny nucleus. A plant comes from a seed. It has its root on earth, and its trunk grows up and up in the air. A river has its source and flows to a larger body of water. In a human body, the inside is the root, outside is the end. All our illnesses begin from the root and then spread to other parts. When we try to cure an illness, we have to decide where to start depending on its seriousness or urgency.

Humans with their intelligence always aim at progress for a brighter future. But when the body and the spirit, which are expressions of Yin and Yang are not in harmony, there is trouble such as illness. For the same reason, a community or a country may be left in chaos.

According to "Nei Jing", "Yin and Yang must be in balance so that our spirit can be calm."

Oriental medicine reasons that the fire, which is Yang from the heart and the fire, which is Yin from the kidneys, must support each other to make our spirit calm. If there is imbalance between Yin and Yang, our spirit will be disturbed, and we do not know which direction to take.

It is the same situation when we are aboard a boat floating without a compass on the high sea and in total darkness. How can we know the direction and steer the boat to the right destination? What will we do if the sky is dark and we do not see the North Star, the moon, or any other stars? In this case we have to calm ourselves, concentrate our mind. "When the heart is calm, the spirit is serene, our head will be clear to show us the essential direction". Only when the heart is tranquil, the energy is calm, the fire of the kidney is steady, are these two important organs able to help each other. Then our spirit will be stable. This is the time when Yin and Yang interact.

Our direction is the macrobiotic way in which our life must be kept in balance and serenity. We have to take responsibility for ourselves, and benevolence has to be the lamp to show the way for us to achieve our goal. "Birth, Old Age, Illness and Death" are natural circumstances we have to accept, share, and sympathize with others. Acceptance of these will make us happy and content.

Human life has ups and downs just as nature has days and nights. In whatever situations we ought to keep balance, distinguish between right and wrong and be able to find the way to progress. We also have to live in accordance with natural law, be happy and humane to others.

Humanitarianism is our way of life. We should not worry about time. In whatever adversities such as darkness, inescapable jungles, or gloomy days, we will always feel serene because we have found the way. Sooner or later, we will see the sun. Therefore, the highest direction for human beings is Humanitarianism. We help one another by sharing knowledge. We should treat others with true love and kindness. Only then can we find happiness in life.

> *"Our body is led by our head*
> *When the road is hard,*
> *We must rely on our heart*
> *As the North Star*
> *To show us the way*
> *We as humans on earth*
> *Must find the "Tao"*
> *That leads to Paradise*
> *The "Tao" is Humanitarianism*
> *That helps us happy*
> *In peace on Earth and in Heaven*
> *Our direction is Humanitarianism*
> *That is bright to all of us."*

vii. Highest Light:

Every one of us knows that the earth we live on is in the solar system

After the 18th century, William Hershel used a telescope to gaze at the sky and knew that the earth is near the end of the Milky Way.

There are other galaxies that are billions of light years away from ours. Because of this enormous distance, we do not know when science can help us visit other galaxies.

People already have paid many visits to the moon. Now they are in the stage of probing Mars. Near our earth there are 8 other planets and the sun whose light brings life to our globe. In our body, there are six "Fu" and five "Zang" (internal organs). Our body's structure can be compared to the universe. According to Oriental philosophy, life is based on the principle of Yin and Yang. In a human body, the brain is considered the sun. The sun gives light to the earth and the brain gives light to us.

Newton and Albert Einstein said that the earth is covered by the radiation of many different rays from galaxies in the universe. These rays contain energetic nuclei that emit electro-magnetic radiation. The earth is also covered by other elements like hydrogen, helium, and oxygen etc. But today's science still cannot explain everything about the universe. Scientists are not sure about a number of galaxies. "The young spiral and elliptical galaxies observed today may thus have formed from the merging of low-mass galactic fragments relatively late in the history of the universe, long after the Big Bang and represent just one of the series of stages in the evolution of the universe." (By Bradley C. Whitmore)

Light and heat that warm the earth come from thermo-nuclear reaction in stars and especially from the sun.

Under the influence of light and heat we have chemical bonds that bind many elements together. One instance of these is water from the combination of one atom of oxygen and two atoms of hydrogen.

We cannot see all the lights that come from the sun and other stars. Scientists tell us that this electromagnetic spectrum includes radio waves, microwaves, infrared light, visible light, ultraviolet light, x-rays, and gamma rays. Visible light, which is only a small part of the electromagnetic spectrum, is the only electromagnetic radiation that we can perceive with our naked eyes. We all agree that light is the source of life, and all human creations must depend on solar light.

Also, under the influence of the light and heat from the sun, the earth has 4 different seasons. According to Oriental medicine, the principle of Yin and Yang is very obvious in the four seasons. The wise men of the past told us to observe and follow the changes of nature to preserve and promote life. If we rebel against nature we will perish.

"The Yin and Yang of the four seasons are the basis of the myriad of things. Therefore, a wise man will nourish Yang in Spring and Summer, Yin in Autumn, and Winter. Follow this fundamental law and you will be on the threshold of birth and growth. Rebel against it and you will destroy its roots and harm its truth. For Yin and Yang and the four seasons are the beginning and end of the myriad things, the roots of life and death. If you rebel against them, you will destroy life. If you follow them, disease will not arise... "He who follows Yin and Yang will have life. He who rebels against them will be dead. Obey and you will be cured; rebel and calamity will follow."

(Su Wen, Sigi Tiaoashen Dalun).

We should also perceive things with our heart. Use our heart to balance the knowledge of the mind. We know that the heart is the house of the spirit. The heart is like the moonlight and should be utilized to balance the sunlight, which is our brain.

From Hindu literature we have these thoughts "The moon's crescent shape was perfect for an ideal resting place after the rigors of earth life." "Adore the sun, rising with all his rays, receiving the obeisance of Gods and demons, the shining maker of light."

In conclusion:

The highest light can be seen as the creativity of the human brain and the benevolence and compassion of our heart. These lights are scientists, intellects, scholars and inventors in arts and technology. We should be grateful for the sunlight that has been giving us life and for scientists and intellects that make our future brighter.

> *"Through the door, light is coming*
> *To bring life to human beings.*
> *It brightens Heart and Mind.*
> *Seasons come and go,*
> *Spring with sunshine*
> *And summer with warm love.*
> *They breathe energy to all species.*
> *Seeds grow and life starts.*
> *To achieve Nature's Balance*
> *We should follow Heaven and Earth's Laws.*
> *Among us we should have Benevolence*
> *As a jewel that gives Light*
> *And Life to all species."*

viii. Highest Earth:

According to Bradley C. Whitmore, "In 1917 the American astronomer Harlow Shapley estimated that the earth's galaxy, the Milky Way was about 100,000 parsecs in diameters, thus providing the first indication of the Milky Way's size. Unfortunately, Shapley neglected to consider the absorption of light from distant stars by dust particles in the Milky Way, which makes objects appear dimmer and hence farther than they really are. The modern value for the size of the earth's visible galaxy is roughly 30,000 parsecs (100,000 light years) in diameter. The Dutch astronomer Jan Hendrikoort found that the sun takes approximately 250 million years to travel once around the center of our galaxy, and he thus was able to calculate that the mass of the Milky Way is roughly 100 billion times the mass of the sun." ("Cosmology", Microsoft Encarta 97 Encyclopedia)

And we know that, "the earth's mass is 5.98×10^{27}g, its mean radius is 6371 km, and its surface magnetic field is 0.31 gauss" (Major Planets, Microsoft Encarta).

All the information above tells us the enormity of the galaxy and the relatively small size of our earth.

Bradley C. Whitmore also told us about the Universe, "According to Gamow's theory, as the universe expanded, the residual radiation from the big bang would continue to cool. By today it should be a temperature of about 3 K (about -270°C/-454°F)."

At such a freezing temperature, no living organisms can exist. On the contrary, an atmosphere with plenty of oxygen protects our planet. The weather is generally mild. There is water and other chemicals. The earth is the only life-supporting planet. Its shape is not a perfect sphere but is slightly pear-shaped and contains many minerals and metals underground and undersea.

In the solar system, the earth is third from the sun behind Venus and Mercury. The temperature in one of the world's hottest regions is 58°C (136°F) in Al Aziziyah, Libya and the coldest place is -89.6°C (-128.6°F) at Vostok Station, Antarctica. The average surface temperature is 14°C (57°F). Next to the earth is its satellite, the moon.

The part that protects the earth is a layer of gases called the atmosphere. The two main gases in this layer are oxygen and nitrogen. The hydrosphere covers 70% of the earth's surface and consists of oceans, seas, lakes, rivers, and underground water.

The rocks in the earth's lithosphere contain many elements. The most abundant is oxygen (about 46.60 percent of the total). Silicon is about 27.72 percent, aluminum (8.13 percent), iron (5.0 percent), calcium (3.63 percent), sodium (2.83 percent), potassium (2.59 percent), magnesium (2.09 percent) and titanium, hydrogen, and phosphorus (totaling less than

1 percent). In addition, there are also carbon, manganese, sulfur, barium, chromium, fluorine, zirconium, nickel, strontium, and vanadium. Also, we cannot forget a powerful force that encircles the earth and is called magnetic field. From "Earth's Magnetic Field, Encyclopedia 97", we have this information, "A powerful magnetic field surrounds the earth, as if the planet has an enormous bar magnet embedded within its interior. The S and N on the magnet indicate the orientation of earth's magnetic field. Because the opposite ends of magnets attract, the northern end of magnets on the earth is attracted to the southern end of the earth's magnetic field, located at the magnetic north. Scientists believe convection currents of charged molten metal circulating in the earth's core are the source of earth's magnetic field."

Scientists also told us that the earth's age is about 4.65 billion years. When the earth was formed, its primitive atmosphere contained carbon dioxide and nitrogen, which were held by earth's gravity. Water vapor condensed and formed the world's first oceans. Heavier elements, mainly iron and nickel sank downward toward the center of the earth.

Besides a lot of minerals and gases, our planet also furnishes us with plenty of essential substances to nourish us and other species including organic matters and vitamins and other substances that were mentioned in the previous part about nutrition. In all, the environment for all species consists of the atmosphere, moderate temperature, land, and water. These factors are necessary for life provided only by our earth.

Now if we look in our body, we will see that it contains the same elements that our planet does. We can also compare the six Fu and five Zang (internal organs) of our body to the solar system because of the movement in the system and in our body. The magnetic force that moves in the earth creates the magnetic field. This force and the gravity help keep us from falling into space.

The composition of our body is the same as that of the earth. We live well as long as the earth is healthy. So, we have to cherish our environment because our body is a microcosm supported and nourished by Mother Earth in the macrocosm of the universe.

We should protect our planet, our atmosphere, and our environment just as we do to our body. We should not harm them in whatever way to cause nature to lose its balance. We should not manufacture any chemical poison to destroy any fellow-humans, any races, or any species.

I am sure that our Mother Earth is grieving and suffering because of her children's wrongdoing. Here, I would like to mention a similarity between nature and humans. In nature, there is the electro-magnetic force that helps it in its movement and existence. In humans, there is also an electro-magnetic force that helps us live and think.

Since each of us is a microcosm in the universe, protection of our living place should be of the highest priority. We should keep our nature in balance so that we, in turn, can have a balanced and happy life. To do this we should keep nature from being polluted and avoid harming or destroying it with disasters and diseases.

Thanks to geniuses like Einstein, we know how to harness nuclear energy and put it into use. But we should use it to serve humans. We should not use it to manufacture nuclear weapons or other chemicals to harm other people or races. To better serve the world we can also use solar energy to create electric power.

We should employ and share our talents to attend to the well-being of humankind. Therefore, I would like to invite all of you to establish a day for the love of Mother Earth to pool our energy and skills to forge a better future for our planet.

We should bear in mind that the earth is just like our body. If we take poisons or toxins into our body, we are doomed to perish. If the earth is polluted or damaged, it is on its way to its collapse. So, we should consider this the responsibility of each of us.

An ancient adage teaches us: "Follow nature and you survive. Disobey it and you die."

"Follow nature," means keeping the balance between Yin and Yang, following natural laws, and practicing man's benevolence and Heaven's way. These sacred principles are inside every one of us, but we have to light the lamp to brighten them ourselves. Here, I would like to invite you to light with me the candle of warm human love to make nature more and more cheerful and lively. Please join me to show our spirit of unity and our sharing of services.

"A Mother Earth's love is immense.
O, Mother I have come back here.
You always care for your young offspring.
Like a mother tending her child
You worry at your baby's first step.
You smile when it walks steadily.
You always say, "Watch out or else you fall."
But time flies very fast.
Your child is already one year old.
And yet you never stop worrying
For you small pear full of vitality.
Your child is the symbol of sacred life.
O, Mother, you give your children your holy spirit
In a paradise full of creativity
The earth is a pear-like globe
That rotates with its sibling planets
And shows its bright light
O, our Mother Earth."

ix. Highest Mouth:

The mouth is the opening where food enters our body. Food then goes to the stomach where it is digested and then turned into blood with the help of the spleen. Blood is stored there and then circulates to nourish the body. Blood is added with oxygen with the help of the lungs and becomes red in the heart. According to Oriental medicine, about the five elemental energies, Water arises from Wood and blood is a kind of water. The liver belongs to Wood. Therefore, blood is stored in the liver. Energy is the master of the blood. Thanks to this energy, blood circulates in our body. The lungs work with the help of energy (Qi) and make us breathe. When we breathe, blood is cleaned and circulates in every channel of the human body.

Oriental medicine also says that kidneys play an important role in the quality of blood. In many patients when kidneys are weak or deteriorate, they cannot help with maintaining the supply of good blood. This situation causes the patients to have a lot of phlegm. Women with low blood counts and troubled menstruation can be cured after the Water element is tonified.

When blood is healthy and plentiful, body muscles can develop.

Old medical books also say, "Blood is the foundation of the body. Flesh is built from blood."

Notes:

Kidneys: two bean-shaped kidneys near the backbone where the point of Ming Men is located. Its black hole in the left is the root of water. Its white hole in the right is the root of fire. Water and Fire are the roots of Yin and Yang and the origin of Energy and Blood and the source of life (Medical book by the great physician Hai Thuong)

Energy and blood are important for the nourishment of the human body. The first act for nourishment starts with the mouth. The mouth is also the origin of life and death.

We need to eat to create energy and blood. These two factors circulate to nourish the body in preservation of life.

The mouth is also the organ that helps us express the thoughts in our mind. Good words with positive ideas can save a person's life. Negative words with wicked ideas can cause a person to die. So, the mouth is the starting point for orders to do good or bad things. In nature the mouth is where a river flows into a sea or an ocean. Thanks to this mouth, people can travel and do business. Even a well where we get water from also has a mouth.

People need their mouths for contact, communication and understanding between countries of the world. Thanks to the mouth we can exchange our knowledge to make life better. The mouth is also the organ with it we can smile to activate the circulation of energy and blood to make our body healthier and our mind more comfortable.

So, the mouth can be considered the source of life for nature and humanity.

"The Highest Mouth, the one that smiles like a flower.
Everything starts with the mouth.
When we smile, we set energy in motion.
In the past many dynasties collapsed

Because of a woman's smile.
A friendly smile can help gather
The world's talents to build a better life.
A smile can warm our hearts
Like the sunshine in a garden of flowers.
Let us assemble our skills and morals
To make the world a safer place to live."

x. Highest Happiness:

Speaking of happiness, every one of us thinks of a situation that we all need and long for our own life.

Then, what is happiness?

When we get what we wish for and when our mind is balanced and happy, then we have happiness.

Whether our happiness is great or small, it always objects an internal state of mind. Sometimes, happiness is only a mental perception without any external object. But in order to be real and lasting, happiness must begin with sincerity, with a true heart or depends on two sometimes with loyalty from both parties concerned.

On a larger scale, happiness can bring a better life to a society or a country. This kind of happiness ought to come from "The True, the Good and the Beautiful". This is a factor: external ways that lead us to an honest and civilized life. But this life requires co-operation, creativity, and equality to make it good and perfect.

First of all, we should start with individual happiness. To achieve this, we have to keep a healthy body. When we are healthy, we are able to do and get what we wish for. On the contrary, a sick person who suffers physically or mentally day or night cannot do anything.

Ancient adages say lots of times about this situation:

"Happy are those who have good eating and good sleeping.
It's like throwing money through the window if you can't eat or sleep."
Or
"Good health is gold."

A healthy body helps us improve our skills or polish up our knowledge. It also gives us favorable conditions to seek happiness. But we should know that happiness is not something remote. It is within our reach because anything that satisfies our mind and heart is happiness. In our social life, happiness is needed for every individual, every family, every community, and every country. To achieve these goals, we must share the spirit of aiming at the positive and the good. With determination and perseverance, we will overcome any obstacles in our life to secure happiness for everybody.

My dear readers, the twenty-first century promises a brighter future and equal peace for the whole mankind. We are determined to unite in our search of peace and happiness for all our family, our society our country and us. This is not a miracle. We can do it if we combine our knowledge, creativity, our true love, and our noble and beautiful ideas. With these factors and the resources from Mother Earth we will prevail over difficulties and achieve the True, the Good and the Beautiful. What we are doing is consistent with humans, with Earth and with Heaven. We will not be afraid of anything because we follow the Tao (Heaven's Way).

Even if we make mistakes, we can correct them because "nobody is perfect" and "failure is the mother of success."

We already know nature's law of the four seasons, and we should persevere in our work.

I would like to call on you for your determination to build a better world for all species as well as for future generations. Open your heart for your compassion to join with other people for the establishment of a new order.

As the ancient sages taught us, "All men from the four seas are brothers"; we should share and learn to improve our knowledge so that we can provide adequate food and clothing to all people on earth.

Happiness must come from a true heart. It cannot be achieved or last long with false feelings. It must come from benevolence and in accordance with our wishes as well as with other people. To be perfect, it must come naturally from our feelings and material factors are only means to make it complete. Its basis ought to be morally sound for each individual.

To attain "the True, the Good and the Beautiful", first of all we have to check our heart to see if we have a noble ideal and benevolence. We must also achieve a balance between material and spiritual factors.

We are all members of mankind, so I would like to invite you to give me a hand working together to build a better life. We need to join our efforts to make a giant circle and share our energy and resources with all people of all races regardless of colors, classes, or religions because we all share the same great religion of Heaven, the Tao. It teaches us to be good people and help us build a bright future for all of us.

We all should thank Heaven for giving us light and Mother Earth for providing us with all the resources to build a good foundation for life. We should also glorify "Humanitarianism" for everybody's sharing and contributions of knowledge and of materials just like the ancient adage that says, "All men from the four seas are brothers."

Then we can rest and contemplate the beautiful crescent on a calm night; "The moon's crescent shape was perfect for ideal resting place after the rigors of earthly life."

"From time immemorial there were the Sun and the Moon.
The Moon changes from new to full.
The Sun is sometimes hidden and sometimes bright.
Just as humans in life
With all its ups and downs
Sometimes there are storms.
Sometimes there is sunny sky.
Just like life's vicissitudes
That makes people sad or happy
But when we are fully awake
With the help of the moon and the sun
We can find the way to our origin.
We are all brothers and sisters
Who share the same ideal.
We are determined to be loyal to one another.
In spite of life's obstacles
We are seeking happiness.
With our true heart

We will attain paradise.
With the help of Heaven and Earth
We can surely build
A world with full happiness."

The happiness that we feel and accept comes from our heart and mind. When we are content with ourselves, we can enjoy a form of inherent happiness. To help you achieve this form, I would like to show you a key to this state. It is the point of Bai Hui (Du.20) on the crown of our head. When it is opened, we will feel comfortable and clear-headed.

Bai Hui is a Yang point. All the Yang energy of the body gathers here. It can be considered a small sun in our body. In cooperation with the heart, it is the source of creativity and also a light to show everything. This point of the Governing Channel (Du.20) is the door to the source of life and of birth. To open this, we need the help of acupuncture.

The point of Baihui (Du.20):
Baihui is the meeting place of a hundred Yang channels. In a human body, there are 14 Governing and Conception Channels. In addition to these, there are other smaller channels. In all, a hundred channels gather at the crown of the head. This point is called Baihui (Du.20), which means "Hundred meetings"

In our body, the heart, the liver, the spleen, the lungs, the kidneys, and the stomach have their functions. The nervous system directs these functions and our mind. These organs and systems control our character, our feelings, and the workings of our body. But finally, all the important channels come together at the crown of our head. When the point of Baihui is opened we have a clear mind, which helps us see and consider everything with clarity. This point is also the crown of intelligence in humans. Once it is opened our intelligence and creativity can develop and increase greatly.

Location:
At the intersection of the median line at the vertex of the head with a line drawn from the tip of one ear to the other.

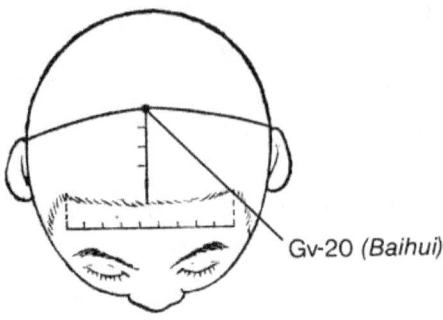

Gv-20 (Baihui)

Traditional Functions:

Clears the senses and calms the spirit, extinguishes the liver wind, stabilizes the ascending Yang.

Traditional Indications:

Headaches, dizziness, shock, hypertension, insomnia, seizures, prolapsed anus (Acupuncture- A Comprehensive Text- Shanghai College of Traditional Medicine- translated and edited by John O'Connor and Dan Bensky).

d. Benevolence – Righteousness – Civility – Knowledge – Loyalty (Confucius):

Do not think it is outmoded or inappropriate for us to discuss the teaching of Confucius here and now right in the free land of the United States of America.

It is my firm belief that you certainly agree with me that a solid and stable house must be based upon a sturdy foundation. Plants enjoy their healthy growth thanks to their strong roots. In nature a tree has its roots, a spring has its source, a bird has its nest, an animal has its den or burrow, and a person has his or her house.

The foundation of humankind, regardless of races, nationalities, social status, or languages, is this planet Earth, our Mother Earth. As citizens of the world, we are all nourished and fed by our own Mother Earth. The earth also serves us, as our common home and, in return, demands us to render her our duty: taking the best care for her.

We must take the best possible care of this earth because it is where we are born, fed, and expire. I do not have the ambition trying to guess the range of our earth's age, possibly billions of years or more; neither is it our main concern here. What concerns us most is how environment, nutrition, culture, and literature can be used to help us maintain natural balance, so we are able to live and grow wholesomely in this modern and civilized world. There must be a balance between body and spirit. A healthy body with a declining, energy-drained spirit indicates the lamp of your life is dying away, and you are at threshold of death.

In order to achieve the natural balance of our life, we need to warmly welcome any spiritual guidance-either ancient or modern. This explains why we include the five following human virtues required for social life as taught by Confucianism:

Benevolence – Righteousness – Civility – Knowledge - Loyalty

These qualities are basic to the establishment of a good life for humans. When a person has learned to become benevolent, righteous, civil knowledgeable and loyal, he can build a happy and peaceful life not only for himself but also for other people.

<u>Benevolence:</u> Each of us may have been taught about benevolence by our elders, depending on the moral background of each family. The important meaning of this quality is that we have to love other people and live honestly. Also, we have to show charity and compassion to all people around us.

<u>Righteousness:</u> Generally speaking, we must have responsibility or duty in life. As an old adage says, "When we drink water, we have to remember its source", we have to have a duty toward our parents because they have given birth and brought us up. When they are old and weak, we have an obligation to take care of them.

These duties encompass many aspects: family, clan, friends, society, country and in a broader sense, the world.

These relations can be mentioned as follows:

- Between grandparents and grandchildren,
- Between parents and children.
- Between husband and wife.
- Between siblings.
- Between relatives.
- Between friends and between neighbors.
- Between people and nations of the world.

<u>(1) Duty toward one's grandparents and parents:</u>
It is our duty to take care of our grandparents and parents when they are old. Although many things have changed in the modern world, we must keep this obligation because everything has its roots. Our civilization will surely decline if we forsake this moral duty.

We all have grandparents and parents. They are our sources or our roots. They take care of us, feed us, and teach us when we are too young to take care of ourselves. It is a duty for us to return what they have done to us when they themselves grow too old and too weak to look after themselves. Doing this is in accordance with the Tao (The Great Way) of Heaven and Earth.

Rain falling to earth from clouds completes a natural cycle: water from earth vaporizes into clouds and finally it returns to earth in its original liquid phase: water. This cycle, like the myriad of other cycles, endlessly repeats under natural law. Humans are no exception: they survive only by their strict observance of this law, the Tao of Heaven and Earth.

When we take care of our parents or our grandparents, we live in accordance with natural law and moral standard. We have to keep this quality because it is morally correct. We should follow what is good in old cultures to make our present life better. We should also teach our future generations to preserve this tradition of filial piety in their social life.

(2) Husband and Wife:

Husband and wife are supposed to share their whole life together, regardless of any ups and downs during their existence. These fluctuations are just as natural like rising and ebbing tides or different phases of the moon. Therefore, in their conjugal relationship, husband and wife are expected to share any joy or sadness together.

We are now living in a relatively peaceful world where separation between husband and wife seems less often than it does in wartime. As a result, some couples do not adequately cherish their union, as they should. They can know the real meaning of union only when they are separated.

Husband and wife should take care of each other especially when one is sick. The more they care for each other, the closer their relationship becomes. Consequently, conjugal relationship is important no matter whatever law (natural or human) is concerned. But this mutual love must be sincere, and the care must be mutual. Doing so we have followed the right way of being a human. I would like to wish that every one of us could live in stable and ever-lasting happiness. How glorious a right human is!

(3) Elders and younger siblings:

Any plant has its roots, branches, leaves, flowers, or fruit. Siblings can be compared to parts of the same tree. These parts share the same nutrients absorbed from the soil by the roots of the mother tree.

This is only an example of small and ordinary trees like orange or tangerine trees. Later I would like to speak of the Universe tree which houses and nourishment nature and all species.

As brothers and sisters, we must share all the ups and downs, happiness, and sufferings in life just as the leaves share the common sap from the mother tree. Nothing is better or more encouraging than fraternal solidarity for mutual well being regardless of where we live.

Vietnamese and world literatures have provided us with many stories glorifying brotherly devotion and care that the elder gives to his younger siblings when their parents are dead.

Today, many changes have occurred in our life. We cannot ask for the same behavior and treatment exactly like it was in the past. But we should always preserve this fraternal love that is full of attachment and assistance. It is one of the noblest images of family as expressed by these sayings:

"A family is the foundation of a society and a nation."

"Only good families can build a good society, a prosperous and stable nation."

(4) Relatives to relatives:

Relatives such as uncles, aunts, nephews, and nieces are also like branches and stems from the same family tree. Besides direct members within a family, we still have blood relation to other relatives. We have to treat and help them with good feelings.

In the past when there were wars, family members were separated or killed. Many of us owed our survival to our relatives like uncles or aunts for their support and protection.

Today, there are fewer wars, but we have to preserve close relations between relatives. We have to frequently pay them visits to make these bonds more secure and to show the noble spirit of solidarity among offspring of the same ancestor.

(5) Friends to friends and neighbors to neighbors:

People usually say, "Close neighbors count more than remote relatives." Indeed, in our life today we see or meet our neighbors oftener than our relatives. These neighbors live next to us. Without them, how lonely and isolated we are!

Sometimes we rarely meet our neighbors because everybody is busy. But whatever level of closeness this relationship may be, we feel comfortable and safe because we know that we have neighbors to rely on. In any emergency, neighbors are most likely there to give us help. That is why we should cherish this relationship.

With friends, we share a large portion of our life: at school, at work or at play. In life, friendship is very necessary for us because it gives us mutual support. Without a friend we often feel lonely. It is proud and lucky for us to have a great friend. He or she is the person in whom we can confide our feelings or our trouble. A great friend is sometimes very helpful in the advancement or promotion in our career or business as expressed in a Vietnamese saying, "A friend can help you with your wealth. A wife can help you with your prestige."

(6) People and nations of the world:

People and nations are members of a great family equal the earth. If we compare our human body with the earth and the solar system, we will see the similarities:

- Human body: the circulatory system with blood vessels to nourish the organs and the nervous system that is related to the human mind.
- Earth: There are many waterways like streams, rivers and oceans moving and connected to underground water channels.
- The Six Fu and Five Zang in the human body can be compared to planets in the solar system. They are always moving just as human internal organs are continually working to keep humans alive.

I would like to say more about these similarities. Many underground water channels are connected to make a great web just like nations assembled to make the world. There is a close relationship between nations similar to the connection between underground water tables.

For each nation, the prosperity and well being of its population depend on the talent and morals of its leaders. If the people trust their leaders, contribute their energy in building their country and if every person joins hands, they can establish a big and happy family.

Here we can pose a question. Why should there be a close relationship between leaders and their people? There will be no prosperity and happiness if leaders and their people do not cooperate in any of their work. Speaking of leaders, if they do not have talents and integrity, the country will be in danger of war or disturbance.

On a larger scale, if all nations in the world unite their efforts, share their scientific and technological knowledge, we can build a safer and happier world and at the same time establish a global solidarity.

Our body has a relationship not only with the earth but also with the universe. Its organs work continuously day and night. Our lungs inhale air from the atmosphere into our body through a vital point. It is the point of Baihui (Du. 20) on our head. It may be compared to an antenna to get in touch with the solar system and the universe.

Our feet touch the earth. On these extremities, there is the point of Yong Quan (Kid.1). It is the principal point of the fire from Yin and Yang kidneys. This point helps human energy and blood get in contact with the earth.

We know that there are water channels moving endlessly underground. Inside our body, every organ is working. The energy and blood are always circulating. They are in contact with other elements in the universe, in the solar system and underground that are also moving.

This mutual relationship between humans and the universe is necessary for our health and survival. Heaven is Yang. Earth is Yin. Humans are the median link between these two poles. As such, humans absorb energy from Yin and Yang and evolve in life endlessly. We always want to have a healthy body, a clear head and be able to enjoy a long life. To achieve this, we have to keep the circulation of blood and energy in our body in harmony with the motion in the universe. We have to keep our mind sound because when the nervous system is in trouble, the blood circulation will be hindered. This hindrance can cause our body to be ill and damage our chance of attaining longevity. It is a duty for every one of us to keep our body and spirit in good shape to enable the contact between Heaven, Humans and Earth. Once this flow of energies operates smoothly, we are entitled to enjoy a long and ever-developed life.

We as humans of the world have a responsibility to contribute our efforts to protect the earth and its water resources for all species.

To conclude, we can say that we need to establish a great solidarity between all countries for the sake of humans' development. To do this, we need to join our hands in a spirit of true humanitarianism.

If we succeed in doing this, our younger generations will have something to put their trust in and all of us will embark on a course to a truly civilized stage in human history.

Civility:

There is an ancient oriental proverb that goes "Let's learn civility first, then literature later." This means that civility takes precedence over academic learning.

Civility is very important in our daily life because it indicates the personality of each individual. A greeting from another person is enough to warm our hearts and give us good feeling toward him or her no matter how familiar he or she is to us. Even a smile without any words spoken is able to make us feel closer and friendlier.

Civility also means ceremonies or rituals that bring order and beauty to our life. Engagements and weddings are some forms of important ceremonies.

Other forms of ceremonies remind us of our ancestors or national heroes whose achievements have benefited us immensely.

Ceremonies and rituals help bring us closer and make our life more interesting through such customs as gift giving or family reunions.

Knowledge:

Knowledge also means mental clarity. The brain is the most important organ in a human body. It is the headquarters of the nervous system that controls other organs. If for any reason the brain stops working, the nervous system may be damaged or paralyzed and worst of all this may result in death. Besides this anatomical aspect, the brain in its mental aspect also refers to spiritual clarity or intelligence. To have mental clarity, we need to have a healthy body and constant learning, research, and practice for individual development.

Mental clarity also requires mental concentration and bodily purification. The training of our mind can be compared to the upbringing of an infant who must be nourished to grow up.

Nutrients to develop an intelligent mind are found in:

- Good books
- Noble images in bibles, books of prayers and good deeds in daily life.

Intelligence cannot become sharp through mere learning and action without stillness. Stillness here means relaxation or rest. Learning (action) combined with relaxation (stillness) results in perfect intelligence. We best develop our intelligence when we are immersed in ourselves in meditation through thinking and mental concentration. In any situation, we need to activate our intelligence. Without it, we cannot progress or succeed in any of our undertakings.

Our mind is like a glass of water. If we put too many things in it, the water will become turbid. But if we let the water stand still and everything can be settled down, the water will become clear. Similarly, if our mind is not clear, we cannot see anything. Then we cannot think or resolve any problems that may occur. Mistakes can happen and the consequences may be disastrous.

Intelligence is necessary in our daily life for:

- Judgment or calculation when we do any job.
- Study to develop any trades.
- Scientific inventions.
- Finding new philosophies to make life better.
- Developing and expressing ideas in arts.

A wise person is the one who knows how to use his brain, his intelligence to blend arts into his life. Do you think arts can enhance the functioning of our intelligence? I think they can. Ideas can be best expressed in musical notes, tunes or lyrics. The value of life can be perfectly increased if we are able to use our intelligence to combine arts with every aspect of our existence. Our intelligence is also our spiritual lamp that will burn forever if we succeed in preserving and maintaining it. It can be considered the natural electric current of our own selves.

Intelligence of great people in human history has left us an immense legacy of knowledge and morals that is an exhaustible source of good examples and learning for us. When we wish to learn to increase our spiritual intelligence, we cannot forget to mention Jesus or the Buddha or other saints.

Each of us has his own likes, his own wishes, or his own way of practice to increase intelligence. One great source for us to train our intelligence is world literature.

We all agree that intelligence is the lamp of our body. So, our body can be compared to a living electric pole that can move, enjoy happiness, or suffer from grief. It is our job to light up our own lamp to show us the right path in life. Whether it is bright, or dim is up to us to decide. For fuel, we ourselves have to supply it with learning from books, bibles, prayers or good deeds.

To develop our life, we need to light up our lamp of intelligence. Children should learn to do this early in their childhood and follow the steps of their elders.

Just as there are days and nights, the lamps of intelligence can be classified as Yin spiritual lamp and Yang spiritual lamp. The highest level of this is enlightenment. Although fate is an important factor expressed by certain external conditions, we are the masters of these lamps and we ourselves can make them bright or dim.

Notes: The Yin and Yang spiritual lamps here mean bad things and the highest level of human intelligence such as enlightenment or the goals of the True, the Good and the Beautiful.

Whether this spiritual lamp is bright or dim, exists or ceases to exist depends on our individual decision. We cannot criticize other people's spiritual lamps because our view or our environment determines our judgment. Each one of us is able to change the Yang spiritual lamp to the Yin spiritual lamp and vice versa.

When we attain the True, the Good and the Beautiful, this level of achievement is called enlightenment. This level requires a lot of learning and practice in order to achieve the balance between the body and the spirit.

Now, what is the key to this level? It begins with concentration and stillness:

- Concentration and stillness of our own mind.
- Stillness of our own wish.

- Stillness of our own action.
- Concentration on our own restraint.
- Concentration on our own time.

Concentration here means meditation, calmness, and purification. To do this, we have to eliminate any bindings and set our spirit free. Orderly arrangement and awareness of sufficiency are also additional conditions that can help lead us to ultimate bliss or highest level of intelligence.

Why are we now not finding happiness but feeling lonely and afraid, and sometimes even losing our spiritual clarity? It is because our mind is wandering and not concentrated. As a result, we cannot attain calmness.

We are influenced by external factors and beleaguered by their complications. Since we have not reached concentration, our spiritual lamps vacillate, and we cannot find happiness.

Another important factor is selfishness. It works against our union and impedes the flow of human electric currents. Therefore, we need to get rid of our egocentric selfishness and support one another by sharing our knowledge and encourage ourselves to be patient. I hope my little heart is able to serve as the first link with other hearts to form a circle of spiritual lamps to light up all corners of Mother Earth. How happy we are then!

Loyalty:

Loyalty means faithfulness or fidelity. Loyalty can be expressed as a tie between our spirit and our actions.

- Loyalty enhances the value of a person.
- Loyalty is a guarantee on our own actions.
- Loyalty is a strong support for our spirit.

Before any writing systems were invented, people had faith in other people's words. That is why we have the ancient saying, "The gentleman is as good as his words."

"The gentleman" here denotes a good person who will go by his words. There is another Vietnamese saying that goes, "A word as firm as a nail fixed in a pole" to show the trustworthiness of a gentleman who will keep his promise even if this may cost his life. So, loyalty can be seen as a noble and sacred personal quality in our daily life.

Today, due to many changes, people cannot rely only on words. Guarantees between humans are more and more based on written contracts, agreements, or warranty documents. Although they have helped keep faith between humans, we should work to keep trust among ourselves to be worthy of gentlemen. To become humans of virtue, we not only should have charity or compassion but also faith in one another. Faith is the starting point to other good deeds that can have a lasting effect.

To conclude, Benevolence-Righteousness-Civility-Intelligence-Loyalty is like a five-colored rainbow that beautifies the sky and helps make life more splendid and noble.

Now I would like to call on your good hearts to join hands with me and with other friends all over the globe to build a beautiful world. We need to use the bright torch from Father Heaven to light up our intelligence and common faith. Mother Earth will be brighter because our electric currents have become more powerful after getting help from Father Heaven and Mother Earth.

"Compassion originates from a kind heart.
Benevolence and righteousness make our piety perfect.
When they are combined
With Civility, Loyalty, and Intelligence
They can light up our torch forever."

e. "Within the four seas, all men are brothers":

This old adage means that all human beings on this earth are closely related like brothers in a family.

To emphasize the spirit of union, a saint taught us this valuable idea that all men are brothers. As said in previous parts, we are all members of the human species although we live in different countries of the world. Differences in societies or nations do not change the fact that we have human blood flowing in our bodies. We have the same emotions, same joys, and sufferings.

Globally seen, we are all attached to and participating in the life of in immense old trees. This universal tree is blooming with many flowers and fruit on many branches. But it also has dry, rotten, or dead leaves, fruit, or branches.

Each one of us is a symbol of each part of this giant tree. We can be a flower, a fruit, a leaf or a root. These items can also be symbols of our hearts and our intelligence: good or bad in our bodies or our spirits.

From the same roots of the mother tree, we get living substances for our individual lives. We absorb innate energy from Heaven and Earth. We drink from the same maternal milk (organic, inorganic substances and water available underground).

Depending on our individual living conditions and personal concept of life, we can give forth-luxuriant foliage, beautiful flowers, and good fruit. But on the contrary, we can produce bad flowers and bad fruit as a result of wrongdoings or wretched principles. All that is the final result of what we have assimilated and worked on. We are responsible for what we take in and for the way we benefit from nature.

To say more clearly, each person is the symbol of a fruit, a flower, a leaf, or a root. Good or bad result depends on our actions and development. The fruit we create may be a delicious one. It may be as splendid as a gem. But it may be a poisonous fruit, an ugly flower or a damaged leaf plagued with devastating insects. Why do we have to take our responsibility?

In the innumerable treasures available in nature, there are good and bad things. In the immense spiritual domain, there are also right and wrong ideas. Each one of us is free to make a choice for him because we are all equal in front of nature.

Who is the person who would not want to enjoy good health, peace, prosperity, and longevity? Every one of us wishes to have a life that looks like a wonderful masterpiece with all colors brought about by us. But we need to have some valuable personality to add to this work of art.

In order to attain this noble ideal, we must nourish beautiful ideas in our minds and carry out praiseworthy actions. We must join our efforts, assimilate, and learn good things from each other to make our lives better. With this spirit of solidarity in our hearts, we will be able to achieve the good life of our dream.

There is a common Vietnamese saying that goes,

"O gourd, be good to the squash although you are of different kinds, you both share the same supporting trellis."

This saying teaches us love and solidarity. These two plants are like us. We belong to different races, languages, skin colors and nations, but we all share our life on the same surface of earth.

The Vietnamese people also have two proverbs that mean the same as "United we stand. Divided we fall."

They go like this "Our strength comes from our union." because "A tree cannot make wood, but three trees can make a grove."

Nothing is better than the spirit of solidarity, "Within the four seas, all men are brothers."

We should humbly thank Heaven and Earth for letting us live together, share our learning and training so that we can make common progress.

Note: The earth has five seas, four seas in this phrase means four directions east, west, south, north.

f. "When you know how to be self-sufficient, you have self-sufficiency. If you wait for sufficiency, when will it come? When you know how to create leisure, you have leisure. If you wait for leisure, when will it come?" (Lao Tse):

This teaching by Lao Tse has a very simple meaning: "We can be happy when we are content with what we have."

In today's modern society, new discoveries in sciences and technology help create a better life. All professions and all fields of work are making progress continuously. As a result, we can never finish learning all of the new things. Sometimes we even have excessive demands, and this will make us suffer a lot.

The majority of us usually want more of what we are having. When we have one, we want ten more. When we have ten, we want a hundred more. In many instances, this greediness seems limitless.

But finally, when we have had what we wished for, we often feel bored or displeased because we had demanded too much.

We should be aware of our limits or the levels of our success. Each one of us has to recognize his relative position and his own capabilities. When we know these things well, we can accept the level of our success. If we know when to stop, we know we have enough. Only then can we live in peace and happiness.

I would like to share with my readers the knowledge of self-sufficiency. Although life is free and human thinking knows no boundaries, we have to set limits for ourselves. For if we abuse our freedom and demand excessively, we can cause us to regret or even suffer to the point of feeling hell in ourselves especially when we misuse material resources. Anything that exists has its own limits. Eating too much food, for example, will inevitably cause indigestion. Pouring too much water into a glass will make it overflow.

This knowledge of self-sufficiency reminds us of the proper moment when we have enough. We must set a clearly fixed limit to ourselves and never demand what is beyond our reach. We can enjoy happiness when we are content with what we are having.

Nowadays, society's morals are degenerating. Human life is in a chaotic situation because of imbalance, of unrestrained freedom and of lack of self-sufficiency. Too much desire and too much greediness for material enjoyment have made us forget our noble spirit. Moral virtues are not cultivated in social life up to a level where they should be. In short, we do not have the spirit of contentment.

When we are not content with what we have and when we lack a real moral basis, we are susceptible to suffering from an imbalance in our thinking. This imbalance will make us feel unhappy. If you consider yourself as having enough of what you wish for, then you are happy. Knowing what is enough to make you happy is the right way to achieve happiness. It is very simple and within our reach.

What I have shared with you until now is like a ripe and delicious fruit. All you have to do is relish it.

"Fruit of my dream, dear friends of mind
I present them to you
Hoping they're enough for you and for me
To live happily in this time of peace
And in never-ending friendship"

g. Educate yourself, Manage your household affairs, Administer your country, then Pacify the world. (Confucius):

In his lifetime, Confucius used to teach people to become good and clear-headed members of a happy family and to establish a stable society, a prosperous country, and a peaceful world. His ethical system was then appreciated and nowadays it is still valuable because his teaching's goals are the same for all of us.

Educate yourself:
If we want to become a good person, first we have to educate ourselves. In order to educate there are two parts:
We have to laboriously gain more knowledge for ourselves.
For our spirit, we have to learn and follow good examples of ancient people to make our life and society better and better and our minds brighter and nobler.

Manage your household affairs:
In managing the household affairs, the head of a family needs to bear in mind these things:
He needs to have a good heart and the responsibility of a good person to be able to take care of his family.
He must perform good actions not only to himself but also to his family and his society.
The head of a family is like a nucleus of an atom. This atom is his family. Many families form a country, and many countries form the world in the same way as atoms form matter. We must follow order or arrangement to make ourselves stable. Then in turn our family can achieve a similar order. When our minds are serene, we are happy, and our family is peaceful. When everybody in a family act in accordance with the order, we have a really happy family.

Administer your country and pacify the world:
Families form a society or a country in the same arrangement as branches, leaves and roots from a tree.
Building a good nation is like building a good family on a larger scale.

When the head of a family succeeds in managing his household affairs well, everybody will be well fed and well clothed. A prosperous and peaceful family is the basis for a stable society. When the society is stable, a nation can be prosperous and peaceful, too.

In building a prosperous country, there must be good leaders. They are also good people who always try to improve themselves mentally and morally. Certainly, these good people take proper responsibility for their families and their countries.

All of us can see that these good things start from a good person and then they will be spread to other components of the world:

- Happy and good individuals
- Stable families
- Peaceful societies and countries
- The happy and peaceful world.

To conclude, we need to learn to improve ourselves, share the above-mentioned good things among us and put them into use to make the world better and better.

2. EUROPEAN CULTURE:

In European literature, there is an expression that I like very much because it fits in with my life and with other people's today.

a. "People of the past used to describe enlightenment as something very great. During the past several months, physical and spiritual sufferings have helped me realize what people of the past meant. Enlightenment is nothing but revelation" (Words by an ancient sage):

If we did not experience any physical or mental sufferings, we would not know what is great. To understand ancient people's thinking and words, we need to learn to reach their true meaning.

In the past several decades, I was being beset by a lot of physical pains. They have helped me with first-hand knowledge that I can share with you here in this book. If destiny had not caused illnesses to befall me in my childhood, I would not have had favorable conditions to know and pursue the medical vocation to help others and myself.

Because of my personal experience, I am able to be fully aware of the physical and mental ordeals that my patients have to endure. I myself had undergone a myriad of pains: soreness in the flesh, smarting in the bones. But the most terrible thing was the mental torment when the head ached and throbbed as if it was pounded with a hammer. The migraine was indescribable and seemed incurable. But I have survived it. These sufferings lasted until the day I came upon Oriental medicine. A number of famous physicians had helped cure my illnesses and in no time, I became their student.

I used to spend my life in a land where fierce clashes between the capitalist and communist regimes have left a painful imprint on my mind. I do not want to talk much about politics because I do not like it. But what I want to mention here are the sufferings that big countries caused to my people and my country. Today I already have medicine to cure my illnesses and to get rid of my agony. The pains that tormented me are now gone. My mental wounds are now healed and only scars are left. The spiritual prescription that I have followed can be used now as a guidebook to share with those who need my help.

In human history, innumerable wars and conflicts have happened to all peoples and all countries. Regardless of races, skin colors or walks of life, many of our ancestors had time and again experienced countless sufferings. When we read a book or watch a film about these events, we can see only the expression of their pains, but we cannot feel them. Only those who were directly involved in these situations could perceive the emotions themselves. Some of these people for some reason could not extricate themselves from their desperate situation. Some of them were clear-headed and calm-hearted enough to find the light to lead them out of darkness. Ancient people called this liberation enlightenment or awakening. It means finding truth and a way of life.

Getting a balanced life back from a deadly situation requires a lot of patience and determination to stand the physical and mental sufferings for a long time. Under our eyes, the achievement made by ancient sages after going through many bodily and spiritual ordeals can be considered greatness. But for these sages, who found their way of life, this achievement was only a way to balance themselves. In other words, we can say that they succeeded in devising a key to their own rescue. Nowadays in our life, we have suffered a lot of miseries and pains physically and mentally. We have to endure the consequences of our actions or even the actions of our ancestors. All these difficulties are building up pressure against our younger generations and us. Do you agree with me that we are now living under serious stress and fear?

The reason for this predicament is our lack of balance. Let us close our eyes and remember what we have experienced. Events in the past will flash back like a movie in our mind. At first there is confusion. But gradually when our heart is calm, we can see things more clearly without any bewilderment. Then we can see the good And bright way of life begins. The redemption lies in our own hands:

"We can become compassionate
When our bodies have experienced pains.
We can only understand others' sufferings

When our minds have endured ours.
We can wake up from our dreams
When our hearts have achieved self-consciousness."

b. "People can live selfishly for themselves, but they must give liberty to other people." (Old adage):

Every one of us wants liberty and usually talks about it. But can anyone among us achieve balanced liberty?

Liberty in perfect balance is an art. I am one of those people who are looking for it. On a fine day after a one-hour noon break in bustling Zurich, I found a big and thick book in the doctor's office where I worked. The book contained many great thoughts from the past. I was curious, so I opened the book to read. I found and liked an expression because it suited my state of mind, "People can live selfishly for themselves, but they must give liberty to other people."

Humans like to be free. They have fought for their rights: freedom of speech, freedom of choice or freedom of thinking. But freedom must be directed to good actions, noble ideas and in accordance with nature's law.

The universe and nature have their own laws. Trees know what is good for their growth and they absorb only appropriate nutrients. Humans know and choose what is good for them. We have to respect and preserve this form of natural freedom. Our freedom must be balanced with good things. We have to choose what is healthy and suitable for our sustenance. We have to distinguish between bad and good to protect ourselves because excessive freedom can harm us physically and mentally.

Humans are the most intelligent animals, and thus we have to choose what is noble and beautiful for ourselves. We have to aim at the Good and the Beautiful in a balanced life. We have to live in conformity with the natural law between Heaven, Humans and Earth. Unlimited liberty can bring us debauchery, suffering and serious diseases. The principle that can help keep us from being ill is moderation and balance.

According to Oriental Medicine, excess in labor or in leisure is likely to result in ailments. There are five chronic diseases that can be caused by:

- Too much sitting
- Too much walking
- Too much reclining
- Too much talking
- Too much looking

In life anything that lacks moderation may be subject to serious trouble. For humans, too much joy or too much sadness may lead to illnesses.

According to Suwen, "Joy injures the heart, anger injures the liver, over-concentration injures the spleen, anxiety injures the lungs, and fear injures the kidneys." (Suwen Ying Yang, Yingxiang Dalun – Acupuncture - Felix Mann M. D.)

In the universe, there is always the presence of two opposing poles in everything: good and evil, bad-smelling and good-smelling, clean and unclean, calm, and agitated, soft and hard, colorless, and multicolored...

Each one of us is free to choose his way of life among these poles. The important thing is we have to take responsibility for our actions. Nobody can criticize your choice because you have your sacred right of freedom. But because we have to take consequences for our choice, we have to think carefully before deciding on our course of action. We also have to take into account the natural law concerning our choice.

"Water has its source.
A tree has its roots.
A fruit has its seed.
A person has his history."

A good tree comes only from a good seed and a good person comes only from good actions. To be stable and happy we have to keep a good balance between our activities and natural law. It is imperative that we have to keep a clear and peaceful mind because "if the heart Qi (energy) is empty, then there is sadness." (Suwen, Benshen Pian) and "If the liver sadness moves into the middle, then it injures the spiritual Soul" (Ling Shu-Benshen Pian).

We all agree that if there are only good things and no bad things, we will not have anything for comparison. If there are no contrasts in life, we cannot judge what is good or bad, frail, or enduring. Opposing things in life teach us a lesson in tolerance and sharing with other people no matter they are good or bad.

Let us read this Vietnamese folk song to see what we want to choose between "the lotus" and "the mud":

> *"In the pond amid the plants*
> *Nothing is as beautiful as the lotus.*
> *Its green leaves are sandwiched*
> *Between white flowers and yellow stamens.*
> *Its white flowers are adorned with*
> *Yellow stamens and green leaves.*
> *Growing in mud, and yet it doesn't smell of mud."*

After reading the song, everybody would like to be the lotus, and nobody will want to be the mud. But we have to mention the truth that the lotus grows and gives out a good smell thanks to the stinking yet nourishing mud. The lotus lives in mud and although it is not dirtied by mud, it cannot live without mud.

In nature there are many instances of this reciprocity. In life we have to accept other people's differences. In order to do this, we have to free our mind of any prejudice, jealousy or hate. We have to give our mind real freedom without any binding. We have to calm down our mind and body. We have to keep our feelings and actions clean.

After we have done this, our mind will be calm and happy.

> *"Every family will be happy forever*
> *Under the lasting and supporting light of Father Heaven.*
> *Everybody will have peace of mind*
> *And a heart full of joy"*

We can do anything for ourselves, but we must let other people have their freedom. We should choose a free life for us but at the same time we should aim at the Good. We should achieve balance without any excess because excess often results in sufferings.

3. AMERICAN CULTURE:

"Walk, balance on Mother Earth. Everything will sit. You make a difference."

One afternoon I was driving my car on the freeway to get home after work. Suddenly my eyes were attracted by a phrase on the back of a car in front of me. I could not read it because the car was weaving fast through traffic. I had to speed up and then I could read the whole phrase that goes like this, "Walk, balance on Mother Earth. Everything will sit. You make a difference."

This phrase described my situation very well because I was learning to walk and keep my balance in life.

The wheels of history are moving continuously and have given us many lessons. Mankind has left both bad and good imprints that we have to accept willy-nilly. We are now inheriting this mixed legacy. There are a lot of things we cannot get rid of. We have to alter and renovate them so that they can fit the relationship between Heaven, Humans and Earth. We have to find a balance in the coexistence of old and new things. There is no need to resort to their abolition. The problem we are facing reminds me of the time when we attended high school. In a lesson in algebra, we had to balance an equation, move the variables to one side or find the common denominator and then we could solve the problem. But balancing an equation in school is quite easy and looking for a solution for a problem in life is not. The difficult thing is that we have to open our hearts to help us get back to our origin and find a common solution to our problem. Only when we have opened our hearts, can we join our efforts to make a better world in the universe system. When different generations voluntarily come back to the origin and share the same direction, we can return to our true heart, our original face, or our childhood heart. Only then can we work out a solution to our problem and form a common web of true hearts that enables us to build a good and beautiful life.

To do this, we have to join our Qi (energy), and start the process of sharing and improving our knowledge to make a difference.

My dear readers, regardless of situations or backgrounds, there is always an understanding between you and I concerning our thoughts and actions. So let us sit down and try to make a difference by achieving a balance in our life and by realizing the motto "Walk, balance on Mother Earth. Everything will sit. You make a difference."

Finally, when germs or impurities infect our present organs, we cannot destroy our body, but we have to cleanse it and try to avoid contaminating our new system. Our system of cells can be compared to a circuit board of tiny electronic chips. We have to clean all these small parts and establish a new system.

We all know that we cannot kill viruses. We can only drive them away or cleanse our body of them. In this case, Oriental Medicine uses the process of catharsis.

IV. THE GREAT SEA OF LOVE

(The Happy World)

Since the creation of the universe with the "Big Bang" explosion, mankind has seen many ups and downs, goodness and evils and constructions and destructions.

From these occurrences we have learned many lessons. In every country's history, there have been countless wars and conflicts for the control of land, people, and resources. Even each individual is competing against others in the struggle for life. But at least all of us are looking forward to a better future. In order to achieve this goal, we need to make a change for the better. Human knowledge is much developed after experiencing many sufferings. But without appropriate moral guidelines the current material progress could spell disaster for the coming generations.

In the twenty-first century we need to have a change to help us attain a perfect balance for the human race. With increasing intelligence, I am sure that we can have a spirit of determination as bright and adamant as a diamond to do this.

We have to learn from the past inventors and scientists who have dedicated their whole existence to the betterment and happiness of our life. Their spirit is still here with us in the books and documents that we are keeping. We have to preserve and revive what is good and discard what blocks or hinders our view. To enhance and put this spirit in practice we need to unite to create love for mankind originated from our true hearts.

We have to keep ourselves healthy and be able to join and work for everybody's well being. We have to broaden our love so that it can become a sea of love for all humans on earth. We also need to be very careful since we have to take responsibility for what we are doing.

For our decision there are two ways of life for us to choose from:

Our red blood can help us have warm human feelings to care for others, be sincere to one another and establish a new source of life for present and future generations. Once this is achieved, the world can enjoy happiness.

But our red blood can also cause us to use force and modern weapons such as chemical and biological types to make wars, fight for resources or kill one another. Then human blood will be spilled all over the earth. The world will become hell.

I would like to mention these two ways because they can lead us to survival or destruction. Therefore, we have to make a wise decision by looking in the same direction and setting up plans for the realization of a happy world.

We all know that when we sow a good seed, we can have a plant with beautiful flowers and good fruit. But if we sow a bad seed, we can have ugly flowers and bad fruit. It is the same with humans' actions. Do not expect good results from bad actions. Appearances cannot deceive anybody. Only results can tell us if our actions are right or wrong.

Just as a farmer harvests the fruit of his sowing, we will enjoy or suffer from what we have done and even from what our ancestors did from the beginning days of the earth.

In a society, people's well being is decided by the actions of the majority of its members. Suppose 80% of the populations of a country do good things, most people could enjoy a fairly happy and peaceful life.

Notes:

Good acts: striving for self-improvement and doing good things to society.

Bad acts: being jealous and greedy, making wars to occupy lands and killing people or doing things that are counter to humanity.

Let us have a look at countries on our earth. We can see the results of human actions. A country that is governed by good people enjoys peace and happiness. A country that is ruled by many bad people suffers from endless wars and famine.

Today the world is also battered by a lot of serious diseases. There are Aids, hepatitis, mental illnesses, and other medical problems without names. The scourge of wars has scared many of us. Our life is not safe because of deadly diseases.

Population explosion is beyond control and has caused a great number of problems such as poverty and famine.

Who is responsible for these troubles? Not only the world leaders but we also have to share the burden of analyzing the problems carefully in order to find a solution.

We all have to take responsibility in world problems and work to preserve the faith in our younger generations. We have to set good examples for our children to follow. Do not forget that we are the most intelligent animals on earth. So, we must learn the lesson in solidarity and unity from the bees or ants that form closely knit societies with well-defined functions for each of their members. Even birds in the sky and fish in the sea know to live and travel in groups to help one another survive. Every animal, even a predator, tries to raise and protect its small ones. Of course, as intelligent animals with noble traditions, we should know how to guard and defend our offspring.

We need to do retrospection so that we can see and enhance our instinct of survival. It is imperative that we have to unite in order to establish a prosperous and happy life for our posterity. We need to work hard to find new devices and processes as well as improve present inventions to better serve our life. We need to erase the painful past, abolish the hatred in our heart and get rid of evil or depraved things. We have to set up new and good things to make up for the material pains we have suffered.

In time, I hope our soul will be appeased and we can become cheerful and happy. We have to look right at our problems and know that only we can save ourselves from any desperate situation. We have to untie what we have tied. We cannot wish for a savior because he cannot save us when the majority of us have done bad things.

Each of us is like a non-husked rice grain. We have to take off the husk ourselves to have a white grain of rice. Even if there is a savior coming to earth, we cannot save ourselves if we do not work to get this white rice grain. The day when the coarse rice grain is husked to give us a white rice grain is the day of real happiness for everybody. These white rice grains will be used as food to make blood and nourish our bodies. They are jewels from Heaven and can be transformed into blood to nourish mankind. To show our gratitude to Heaven, we should use our warm blood to form a sea of love for all human beings in the world. Our choice is true and in accordance with the three elements: Heaven, Earth, and Humans. It will bring about our rescue, preserve our continuity and create a happy world.

The great sea of love: The day we achieve this will be a day of genuine freedom and of greatness made by our own choice. The pot of cooked rice has become a reality thanks to everybody's labor. We are happy because it will be transformed into a flow of blood to nourish our body. Everybody has to make his or her own rice. This means that we have to improve ourselves and train our characters in order to become good people.

We should glorify this great sea of love with real progress and civilization, equality and a new system established by bright and happy ideas from our hearts.

We should set up a day of Heaven by joining our hands, walking along the bright path and initiate a new system. We will cheerfully share our Mother Earth among us and change this globe into a paradise where we can live in perpetual happiness.

All this is not a dream. It is a reality! When my hands are in yours and when my ideas are exactly like yours, our "Yin and Yang" are in perfect balance.

Let us march forward to our great day. Let us do noble acts and bring about happiness to everybody. We need all your help for our present and our future.

God has given us two choices:

(1) The end of the world: We can destroy ourselves with negative, dishonest, and deceptive dealings because they will eventually bring about imbalance, inequality, chaos, wars, and a serious decline in our morality.
(2) A paradise on earth: We can live in a lasting paradise with sincere sharing originated from our true hearts. Science with appropriate morals will create a happier and more beautiful life for all of us.

Let us speak clearly and loudly that we take the second choice. Our true hearts will be glorified. Our lights will shine brightly alongside the sun and the moon so that each individual, each family, each community, each country and the whole world can share the common joy. How sweet it is!

The seeds of the love are sown all over the world. If our dream has come true, the warm sea of human love will take the place of devices of mass destruction like nuclear or biological weapons.

This is a gift from God. God is in our hearts and our minds "All for the real human love."

In every corner of the globe, everybody will feel no more fatigue or mental pains. Like a miracle, our souls will be freed from worry and stress.

Before we can make a decision, we need to have a clear vision. The great sea of love can be achieved only when we see clearly with the opening of our third eye. It is the point of Yin Tang. This point gives us the utmost clairvoyance. It is the eye of our spirit that helps us perceive things distinctly and do thing well and precisely. With the help of our mind, our eyes can see more clearly.

The point of Yin Tang is the eye of our soul. It can help us have a lasting and peaceful life.

The point of Yin Tang:

Yin Tang means, "Seal Hall"

Location: It is at the mid-point between the two eyebrows.

Traditional functions: It eliminates Wind Heat and calms the spirit.

Traditional indications: The opening of this point can cure headache, vertigo, common cold, hypertension, insomnia, and infantile convulsions.

(Acupuncture, Shanghai College of Traditional Medicine)

"In our body, Seal Hall is the important point.
It helps open our magic eye.
It increases our intelligence.
And brightens our human heart.
When we open our beautiful eyes,

We will see the right way of life!
Nothing is happier than a peaceful rest.
Let us get rid of any worry
And join our efforts
To spread the great sea of love
That brightens all the sky.
O, happiness, where does it come from?
It comes with the opening
Of all our hearts
When we really care for others,
Our life will become a paradise.
We will harvest the ripe fruit
That we jointly grow.
With our lasting blood and energy,
With our wholehearted cooperation,
We will make the great sea of love
Spread to all continents of the earth.
Happiness will fill our body and soul
Like the rising tide that never ceases."

V. PRACTICE

The important thing now is how to put in practice the facts and theories that we have been discussing in this book.

As an ancient saying goes, "You should try your best before you can know God's will", we have to do all we can before we stop and wait for God's disposition.

If you all agree with me on the balance that I put forth on these pages, let us open our hearts; exert our charity and benevolence to make it a reality. We need to arrange things in good order and unite our efforts to establish a new system.

If you decide to follow my plan, let us jointly remove the husks from our rice grains with joyful and voluntary intent. Lasting happiness is possible only when we work cheerfully, comfortably and without any obligation. When we put our plan into practice, we need to have two basic factors:

"Good health is gold"
"For the mind to work, the body must have fuel"

We all know that we need to have a healthy body and a sound mind to do our work. Good health is closely related to proper clothing and wholesome food. These are the two essential factors that are needed before we can carry out our plan. My dear readers, we are all members of a great and happy family of the world. Let us join our efforts to build a new life with equality and order.

Our cooperation must be based on equality because without it our activity may fall into disagreement and chaos. Even when we achieve success in our work, inequality could cause it to collapse very easily.

When we use all our energy and resources, we do not want to spend them for nothing. We want to harvest the fruit of our labor. We have to use our pot of rice properly. We are not to squander or destroy it because it represents our efforts to produce essential food. We also have a responsibility toward our posterity. We do not want them to bear the consequences of our waste or our destruction.

In order to live a happy and productive life we need the help of a particular point in our body that I am going to show you. This point lies in our hands. Our hands are the tools of creation. Although they are small, our hands are carriers of our strength. They have helped us build our great and happy world for everybody to enjoy.

This point is called the point of Laogong (P.8) Labor's Palace. This term means that our hands are the place where our work or actions originate.

<u>Location</u>: With the finger cupped in the palm in a half fist, this point can be found in front of the tip of the middle finger between the 2nd and 3rd metacarpal bones.

<u>Traditional functions</u>: The opening of this point cure chest pain, inability to swallow food, jaundice, hand tremors, "swan hand", madness, ulcerated oral cavity, coma from stroke, heat exhaustion, angina pectoris, stomatitis, frightened fainting among infants, hysteria, mental illness, excessive sweating of the palms, numb fingers.

(Acupuncture-Shanghai College of Traditional Medicine)

"Although they are small and humble,
Our five fingers are like five mountains
That can touch clouds in the sky.
They contain immense power
That helps us achieve greatness.
They provide everybody with ample food
And warm clothes to make us healthy.
Thanks to our working hands
Our body is strong, and our mind is sound.
When we wholeheartedly join our hands,

We can bring about peace and prosperity
To any place in the world.
When all of us really unite
We'll all enjoy happiness and liberty.
Let us join our hands
To enter our life's palace
Let us make a bright fire
To cook our pot of sweet-smelling rice
Which represents our sharing of love
And our spirit of equality and fairness
Let us thank our Father Heaven
For giving us favorable weather
Let us thank our Mother Earth
For giving us bountiful crops
Let us join our hands
To create peace and love for all."

Notes:
Palace = The point of Laogong (P.8) (Labor's Palace)

P.8 *(Laogong)*

I would like to tell more about this point. It belongs to the Arm Absolute Yin Pericardium Channel.

If we want to have good results, our action must originate from our heart. In life we often have two ways to choose from, the good way and the bad way. We all know that the good way with good actions is always glorified.

If we want to achieve good deeds, we need to have cooperation between the point of Laogong and the point of Hegu (Equal Adjoining Valleys). This point belongs to the Arm Yang Brightness Large Intestine Channel.

The teamwork between the Yin (Laogong) and Yang (Hegu) Channels helps us clearly see the right way for our actions.

The point of Hegu (LI. 4): "Hegu" means "Adjoining Valleys". It helps or cooperates with other points such as Laogong to bring about better results.

Location: With the thumb and index finger extended and stretched apart, this point can be found slightly to the index finger side of the area between the 1st and 2nd metacarpal bones.

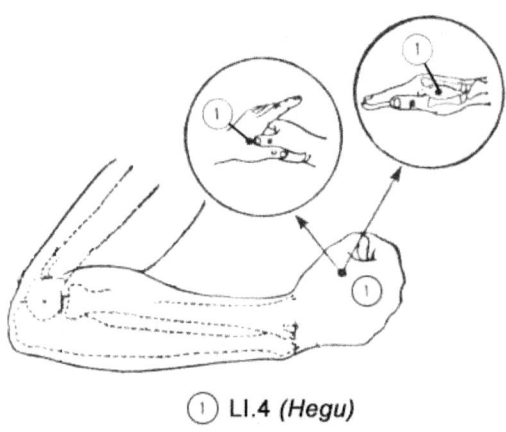

① LI.4 *(Hegu)*

Traditional functions: This point can help disperse Wind, relieve Exterior conditions, suppress pain, and clear the channels.

Traditional indications: Once stimulated, it helps cure headache, common cold, pain in the eyes, nosebleed, deafness, toothache, facial edema, throat blockage, mouth and face awry, hemiplegia, neurasthenia, "locked jaw" due to stroke, tidal fevers, scabies, aborting dead fetus.

(Acupuncture- Shanghai College of Traditional College)

"When we cannot break a bunch of chopsticks,
We remember the old lesson.
A bunch of chopsticks is unbreakable.
But one single chopstick can be easily broken.
The lesson is "Unity makes strength".
Even if the mountain is high
And the sea is infinitely large,
We can achieve our goal
If we all join our hands
We can make our dream come true
If our hearts beat the same rhythm
Our Father Heaven will be pleased
If we unite in loving solidarity
And share our food and clothes
In lasting peace and happiness."

VI. THE BRIGHTNESS OF THOUGHT DETERMINES THE FINAL DIRECTION OF THE HEART:

"Fate" has brought us together and given me the opportunity to guide you through many pages and stages. Eventually we cannot avoid saying good-bye to one another. But such is life: "union and dispersion." We certainly hope there will be "reunion".

Ancient people used to say, "It is hard to fully understand all the books we read." But in this book, I am sure that it is not difficult for you to understand its meaning. In order to cure our own illness, we need to find out the sources of our medical problems. In the first part of this book, I already talked about the importance of the spirit factor: "Spirit in peace, longevity will be attained. Spirit in pieces, body will be ruined."

Many illnesses are caused by the state of the spirit. According to Oriental medicine if the Qi (energy) and blood are weakened, there will be many illnesses. The ancient medical book "Nei Jing" says, "When we know the important point, one word is enough. When we do not know the important point, no words can help." In another medical book, there is this phrase, "When we cure the source, other illnesses will disappear." The important fact is the Yin and Yang of the Qi (Energy and the blood).

The essential Qi of our body can be damaged or sickened by bad Qi (poisonous gases, microbes, or bacteria). All these teachings tell us that we need not only cure physical illnesses but also mental and internal illnesses. We have to find and cure the source and not only the symptoms. When we cure internal pains or illnesses, all other diseases will go away.

Only you can cure your internal pains. I can help you with my advice. To do this, we need to establish a force using Pranayama and Akaska (matter) available in nature to achieve our goal (please see the part about "Breathing" again)

In order to have good results, we need to consider the following guidelines:

(A) Everybody needs to build a healthy body and a sound mind. We need to open the points and chakras in our body to preserve the seven elements related to our life:

- Earth
- Water
- Fire
- Air
- Sound
- Light
- Thoughts and ideas

Those are basic factors that constitute human beings.

(B) We need to keep our families and ourselves cheerful. We need to share our knowledge and resources with other people on the way to establishing a paradise.

(C) Our goal is ascension or to aim at good things as discussed in the part of the Ten Highest.

- We have to achieve equality in every field for family's, society, countries and ourselves.
- We have to ennoble our thoughts. We have to be voluntary and wise. We must not be selfish and jealous. We must not be factional, fanatic and superstitious.
- We have to use love to cure any mental illnesses for other people and ourselves.
-

(D) For practice, we have to apply the "Spirit of Benevolence."

- Benevolence is essential for us, for everybody and for all species. Without benevolence we will lose everything, even our soul. Lack of benevolence may result in suffering for us, for our families and other people.
- The spirit of Benevolence should be glorified because it represents human morality.
- The spirit of Benevolence should be lifted to become a revolutionary movement of Humanitarianism for all coming generations. It is the way leading to the golden goals of "The True, the Good and the Beautiful."
- The True: An honest and happy life.
- The Good: A kind and tender heart.
- The Beautiful: A bright and harmonious balance. Once these goals have been achieved, we can have very positive results.

When our spirit is calm, Yin appears. When our body exercises regularly, Yang is strong. These two elements will help us enjoy longevity.

We need to serve everybody with equality because without it everything will be in chaos.

When Benevolence is accomplished, mankind can attain a balance between Yin and Yang and realize a paradise on earth.

When Benevolence is accomplished, we have built the base to march toward a progressive and happy world.

(E) We need to learn and share the fine cultures of the world: Asia, Europe, America, and other continents in a spirit of members of a great family whose mother is the Earth.

We need to protect the earth just as we protect ourselves. This is the way we, as the most balanced and intelligent animals, express our gratitude to Mother Earth. We can do so to the mother of all species by protecting the Earth just like we protect ourselves and by exercising and developing the noble title that God has given us by showing our highest responsibility toward the Earth. We also have a duty to preserve equality among us in any field of work in society.

(F) Develop our intelligence regardless of different fields of work. Any walks and any professions in society have to treat one another with equality and benevolence. We need to learn and share our knowledge to raise the standard of living. We also need to unite to build a better world.

Our environment needs to be kept clean so that our health is not harmed by pollution. Our goal should be equality and freedom for mankind in a natural order and sincere benevolence in the light of the sun, the moon, and the stars. All of these are symbols of a true heart and a bright mind.

We need to recognize the Yin and Yang parts in ourselves. We need to minimize the conflict between capitalism and communism by being impartial to any of these two different theories. We should consider Humanity the best solution to the chronic scourge of wars, hatred, and genocide.

Only true human love can help us get rid of these morbid mentalities. Yin and Yang have combined to cure all things on earth. But our problem is that mankind has thought up many ways to compete, fight and kill among humans and endangered the process of evolution. The causes of these problems are:

-   Selfishness, arrogance, fanaticism, and superstition. The only way that can lead us in our evolution is natural and pure light. Without "Yang" we cannot enjoy longevity or maintain everlasting existence. Without "Moderation" and "Equality" we would condemn ourselves to self- extermination. To correct these defects, we need to exert moderation in solving our problems or modifying any theories that lack balance. Only "moderation" can help us understand the Yin and Yang in our body so that we can solve our problems or erase imbalances caused by different philosophies or theories that have led mankind to many senseless massacres.

Our intelligence is the light given us by Father Heaven. It helps us cherish and respect life. If we do not cherish life, we are no more than mindless animals. Even if we follow capitalism or communism, it is only a matter of names. Careful analysis will show us that the wrong philosophy is the one without Humanity. Any philosophy should originate from our Heart and the name is not important. Any theory that does not contain Humanity will result in resentment, opposition, and incessant wars. No matter what theory we follow, we must not have any ideas of stealing or robbing labor or wealth from other people. If we harbor any of these ideas, we are affected by individualistic selfishness.

For example, a rich person and a poor person live together. The rich one relies on the other's labor, the poor one relies on the other's wealth. If these two people intend to steal from each other, they would cause a kind of atheistic communism on atheistic capitalism to exist. Even if we use any name to hide or provide excuses for our thinking and action, the origin is still egoistic individualism.

This mental state will cause us to care only for us and to lose our true heart and wisdom.

When we try to cure an illness, we have to analyze thoroughly to find its causes so that we can administer the right medicine.

In the light of Oriental Medicine, I have a responsibility to examine and analyze our thoughts to find ways to save our posterity and to show the curing method to any of us who want to cure our own mental problems. After we have known the causes of our problems, we need to get rid of them. Otherwise, mankind's progress will be stopped, and wars will happen without any letup.

To cure our own illnesses and share knowledge with other people, we need to help mankind to march toward a brighter future. I do not profess any theory or philosophy. I only propose the idea of balance. We need to follow the path of our Heart, see Yin and Yang clearly and practice the right way of Humanity. I offer this as a small lamp to:

- All mankind and as an act of gratitude to Father Heaven, and Mother Earth and my parents as mentioned on the beginning pages of this book.

I hope that the equality of human rights will be restored in a framework of natural freedom and that the light of Yang will be glorified as the result of our work.

I would like to say more about the "Seven Emotions" to help keeping ourselves in balance. If we are not able to control ourselves, we will be overwhelmed by emotions, and illnesses may result.

- We must not get overjoyed because this excess will damage the heart and the pulse will become weak (too much joy results in fever). The ancient medical book "Nei Jing" says, "Excess of joy will damage Yang. Excess of happiness will damage the Vital Spirit." Too much joy can increase fire in the heart.

- We must not be overpowered by fear because it will damage the kidney, the gall bladder, and the pulse will become agitated. Fear occurs while eating may harm the spleen and the stomach.

- We must not let our anger explode because it will damage the liver, and the pulse will fluctuate like the vibrating cords of a musical instrument. Too much anger may harm the Yin Qi.

- We must not be subdued by extreme care because it can damage the lung. Then Qi will be blocked, and the kidney will be weakened.

- Too much pity may injure the pericardium of the heart. Then the pulse will become fast and the spirit in disarray because the two elements Fire and Water are in conflict.

The medical book "Nei Jing" says, "Too much grief may harm the vital spirit." As humans, no one among us can avoid being affected by the seven emotions. We must try our best to control ourselves. We must not let ourselves be overwhelmed by sadness, joy, worry, anger, love or hate. In the case of sexual desire, we have to be moderate to preserve our vital energy and keep our bones strong. Every one of us knows that indulgence in this desire will harm our body and spirit. If we want to enjoy a long life, we need to practice moderation and live-in harmony with nature. This way of life will help us have a healthy body and a sound mind.

About desire in general, Lao-Tse said "If we don't see anything that stimulates our desire, we can keep ourselves undisturbed." In life we need to take good care of our vital energy. When our spirit is steady, we can enjoy longevity. When our spirit is lost, our body will perish. We need to nourish our spirit, nurture our True Yin and True Yang by keeping our heart calm and peaceful.

For conclusion, the formula for a healthy body and a sound mind is balance, control of one's True Heart and moderation.

All of us have things in our body or mind that need to be corrected or improved to make us better. What we need for our present and future is balance. We have to clean our body and spirit to welcome the Good that will come from our own hands. We must use the red blood in our True Heart to achieve a great sea of love for our new life with lasting peace, freedom, and happiness.

Only we can rescue us from any dangerous situations and develop our civilization and progress to create a better life. For effective work we must set up a joint system. Then our labor will be rewarded with prosperity, peace, and happiness. We can be the masters of our own destiny with ample humanity, energy, and intelligence. We will be able to establish an education that puts equal emphasis on physical and moral values. Lastly, we need to wholeheartedly unite and look in the same direction of the Good with our entire fervor.

The successful realization of this new life depends largely on our posterity who must show the highest level of agreement in their task.

Happiness or hell on earth is up to us and all our posterity to decide. Then what makes a hell for us?

- Deceit
- Rampant crimes, drug abuses and depravation.
- Greediness for material things, loss of conscience
- Control by money
- Loss of purity in life
- Loss of faith and lack of direction for younger generations and their risk of becoming false intellects in society.
- Our fire of life goes out because our True Heart is lost. Pure spirit cannot be preserved.

A person without conscience and perspicacity is no more than a walking ghost.

Paradise or hell is now in our hands. It is up to us to decide to build or destroy this world. We need together the power from the nucleus of our hearts and our magnetism to form a kind of solidarity as strong as nuclear force. We need to open our hearts and join our hands to create a mighty force to build a prosperous and happy life. God will be embodied in each one of us with bright light to dispel the mighty darkness.

The brightness of our lamp will form a new existence with the start of the fire of life. It is the Sun, the Moon and the Stars that show us the way to "The True, the Good and the Beautiful" in an everlasting happiness.

> *"The fire of love is brightly burning.*
> *To make life more worthwhile*
> *Let us light up our lamp*
> *To show the radiant side*
> *Of creation in our existence*
> *We unite and work hard*
> *To achieve good health and prosperity*
> *For everybody in the world*
> *Mystery, ignorance and confusion*
> *Is no more blocking our view?*
> *I'd like to thank Heaven*
> *For giving us light to brighten*
> *This life of ours on earth*
> *O, God, you have led us*
> *To the Good and the Beautiful*
> *With everlasting peace and happiness."*

And this perpetual lamp from the beginning of life will be glorified:

VII. CREATIVITY FOR OUR OWN RESCUE:

The greatest human natural instinct is survival. But nobody can escape natural laws. Recycling is one of natural laws that help us survive and develop. We need to learn to live in harmony with nature. If we are acting against natural laws, our destiny will be at risk.

In nature, there are small and large springs, small and large rivers, small and large seas, and small and tall mountains. Among humans, everybody is equal. But our intelligences are different because of each individual's ability and interest in learning.

There is an old saying that goes, "You reap what you sow." This teaches us to be careful in what we do. Good fruit or bad fruit depends on our planting. We have to accept the result of our actions. If we fail, we should consider it a lesson for improvement. We learn from our mistakes to avoid them and do better later on. We should know that "Failure is the mother of success."

There are ups and downs in our life, just like ebbing and rising tides in nature. After times of calm or stormy weather we realize that "You flourish if you follow Heaven's laws. You perish if you are against Heaven's law."

We learn from many lessons in the past like the rise and fall of a myriad of dynasties. They can help us be able to rescue ourselves. What we need to do is to try to balance our life in the current situation and create good and useful accomplishments for us and future generations.

Human harmony, which is the necessary condition for us to make progress, is also in conformity with Heaven's Way. Heaven's Way is the indispensable lamp that showed us the eternal life. It is the way of humanity regardless of races, languages, or religions. It is the natural law of Father Heaven and Mother Earth.

Every one of us is equal in the natural balance because "there is Yang in Yin and there is Yin in Yang." We lose this balance when we become selfish and blind because of our "ego". Indescribable sufferings in human history are sufficient proofs for us to wake up and rescue ourselves.

We cannot do anything against Heaven's laws. Those who are wise always follow these laws. We need to live in harmony with the three elements: Heaven, Earth, and Humanity.

The sages of the past advised us much about these relations, "If you understand above, the writings of Heaven (Astronomy); below, the principles of Earth (Geography), and in between Heaven and Earth, the affairs of man: then you may have long life."

When we try to cure a patient, we also have to pay attention to nature's laws, "If in curing the sick, you do not observe the records of Heaven nor use the principles of Earth, the result will be calamity." (From "Yin Yang", Ying Xiang Dalun and Zhu Zhijiao Pian)

When we have achieved the harmony between Heaven, Earth, and Humans, we can enjoy a long life.

- The Way of Humans is Benevolence and Equality.
- The Way of Heaven is Harmony.
- The Way of Earth is Order and Balance.

This harmony will help us preserve and strengthen the Yang energy. It will help new life such as new buds or plants in springtime.

The origin of life begins with the Great One and the Infinite One (Yin and Yang), and with energy from the Sun, the Moon, and the Stars. In science we know that nuclear energy comes from atoms of the elements.

Thanks to technological progress, the electronic communication web has been set up and has brought us closer. This system has helped us learn and exchange knowledge quickly all over the world. But we need to be careful because if bad images and ideas are spread, the consequence will be very damaging to our future.

We all know that if we want to have a white rice grain, we have to husk it ourselves. If we want to build our future, we need to work for it. If we love our children, we must take the responsibility to educate and protect them. They need the true love from their parents and grandparents. We have to form a good and favorable environment for their development. In order to have good human beings we must help them have good health, talent and right moral conduct to lead future generations.

When our children know that they are protected and given good examples by us, they will have faith in their elders and in life. They will try to become good people like their elders. Therefore, good deeds are our responsibility if we want our posterity to be able to avoid ignorance, sufferings, and endless conflicts.

All of us shall agree that our generation has gone through too many physical and mental pains. This experience has given us enough information to teach our children.

Human history has left us many precious lessons. We have to avoid past mistakes and use these lessons as a foundation to build our civilization with a balanced and perfect life. The Sun has risen after so many gloomy days. This Sun will brighten our new life for us and for our young generations that share these factors:

- Sincere love and unity with responsibility for all humans.
- Everybody is equal in a balanced environment.
- Our actions are done on a basis of free choice and voluntaries.
- Our creativity is used to create material and spiritual conditions to serve and glorify mankind.
- All walks and professions in society wholeheartedly join their hands to establish a better life.

Only with our own hands can we build a propitious way to preserve our spirit. We need to realize our responsibility and work to develop a clean and healthy environment. We need to get rid of the past that has burdened our hearts and given us endless mental pains and other illnesses. We need to dispel it so that we can look forward to a new life. We need to do it for our own rescue.

My dear readers, I am your sincere friend and fate has brought us together in this book. I wish to be your spiritual friend who would follow and support you from now on. I will share with you any concern or worry that may appear in your mind. Please believe in my words because I share the same heartbeat and life rhythm with you. We as humans have very powerful perceptiveness. It can help us understand one another with our faculty of telepathy.

Leaders of a group, a country or a big union usually care for their followers, but there are too much pressure on their life and their work. They cannot establish a good system by themselves. They need everybody's assistance to create happiness for a community, a society, a country, or the world. We do this work not only for ourselves but also for our posterity. Nothing will be better if we set good examples to our children with our own actions. We need to join hands with our leaders to perform good deeds and help reduce the numbers of wrongdoers. As a result, families and society in cooperation will decrease the construction of prisons because of the right and wholesome education with our leaders. Those who go astray will see the good deeds by their leaders and eventually they will realize their errors. They will try to follow the good examples, right their wrongs and build a new and better life for themselves.

To rescue other people and ourselves we need to have noble thoughts and ideas from ourselves and from our clear-sighted leaders who really care for everybody.

Our self-rescue depends on ourselves and on our leaders. We need cooperation and unity to establish a good system just as in the universe; every matter has its own system consisting of numerous atoms with a nucleus in the center and a group of electrons revolving around it. When we have achieved a perfect balance, our future will be brighter. I wish that mankind would succeed in forming a much-needed harmony with Heaven and Earth.

Our dream will become true when there is sincere cooperation between individuals, societies, and countries in the world.

We need to join our hands and souls to set up a new system in which everybody is in charge of one function like that of an electronic web.

With the help of God, we can enjoy lasting peace and happiness because He is the powerful light, the new source of life and the endless beautiful creation.

We have to clean our body and spirit for our own rescue. God's bright light is in front of us. Just look up and we will see His light. The new life is like a rainbow with its beautiful colors. Our body will become healthy, and our mind will become sound to welcome peace and happiness.

We have the freedom to make a choice about our rescue. When every organ in our body is in good shape and our mind is peaceful, our life is balanced. It is then as beautiful as a rainbow in the sky.

Heaven, Earth, and Humans are now in harmony. We, humans, are able to develop forever. The Balance of Nature is now established everywhere on earth.

"In the grain of rice there lies our destiny
As pure as jewel bestowed by Heaven.
Today we have known the secret.
Life is built with our own hands.
From the grains we have a pot of rice,
Like jewels bestowed by Heaven.
We have freedom and independence
Handed down from our ancestors.
O, Humans, life is so immense
With comfort, peace and happiness
We have the keys to all these doors.
Let us open our hearts.
To welcome the spring wind,
With its warm, golden sunshine
Thanks to harmony among people
Prosperity and peace can be blossoming."

Angeline Lan Doan, O.M.D.

ABOUT THE AUTHOR

Angeline Lan Doan has practiced acupuncture, traditional Oriental herbal medicine, and alternative therapies in Vietnam, Switzerland and the United. In 1980 she traveled to Switzerland where she worked as an acupuncturist in the offices of Dr. Christen Theo, M.D. and Dr. Paul Tobler, M.D. in Zurich. In 1985, she came to the United Stated where she went into more studies in both master and doctorate degrees in Acupuncture and Oriental Medicine at South Baylo University in Anaheim, California. She is also a diplomat of the National Certification Commission for Acupuncture and National Certification Commission for Acupuncture and Oriental Medicine (NCCAOM) in 1989 and a member of California Acupuncture Association (CAA).

In the year 1989-1997, she worked as a therapist and herbalist in Chiropractic Medical Center in Woodland Hills, California. She invented an herbal formula called "CerviCordy Energy" and did collective research to write this book "Balance of Nature". She successfully healed herself and helped many patients at Century Medical Group in Van Nuys, California. She tried to achieve balance both in physical health and mental health in her life. She has wakened the Truth, the Goodness, and the beauty in her and people around her.

Her "CerviCordy Energy" herbal supplement helps to balance Tang Fu (organ system), nervous systems, promotes energy, restores sexual functions in men and women, restores health for people with stress, chronic fatigue syndrome, paralysis, recovers health after strokes, help people with memory decrease.

Her "Balance of Nature" book published in Author Reputation Press, LLC. brings up the Truth and shows how we can harmonize healthy spirit and physical body between Heaven-Man-Earth that will benefit, long good life in reality.

More about the Author:

She is Doan thi Lan known as Lisa Lan Doan / Angeline Lan Doan, alias Hong Ngoc Chau. Born in the village of Dieu Hoa, My Tho, Dinh Tuong Province on the 16th of June 1954. Her parents' names are Doan van Tuoc and Mui Vuu (Vưu Phung Anh).

She worked for the Administrative and Financial Service No. 7 from 1971 until 1975. From 1976 to 1979, she studied and graduated from two courses at Tien Giang University's branch, one in Medical Acupuncture and the other in Pharmaceutical Acupuncture. (Tien Giang University's Institute of Medicine and Pharmacy's Professor Truong van Boi) She sought for asylum in another country on April 9, 1980, and arrived in Kuala Lumpur, Malaysia, on April 30.

Arrived in Geneva on July 21, 1980. From 1982 to 1985, she worked in the Zurich, Switzerland office of Dr. Christen Theo and Dr. Paul Tobler. From 1986 to 1989, Attended and graduated from Traditional Acupuncture School at South Baylo University, California, USA. From 1996 to 1999, Convalesced and did research for writing "Balance of Nature" / "Can Bang Cua Thien Nhien" and prepared "CerviCordy Energy" herbal supplement. From March 3, 1999, she worked at Century Medical Group in Van Nuys, California, with Dr. Denise Anh Duong Phan.

Fruits are her favorite. Traveling, sports, natural arts, and social services are some of her best hobbies to do. Music, painting, and poetry are her strong points. She wishes for more social activities. There will be no more sufferings from wars, genuine independence, equality, and love among mankind, as well as benevolence in life.

BIBLIOGRAPHY

Reference books and documents:

-   Acupuncture, the Ancient Chinese Art of Healing and How It Works Scientifically - Felix Mann, M.D.
-   Acupuncture, A Comprehensive Text, Shanghai College of Traditional Medicine.
-   Vietnamese Medical Book.
-   Hai Thuong's Medical Principles - Lan Ong Le Huu Trac.
-   Nutritional Therapy - Nguyen The Thu, D.C.
-   Nutrition Cultism: Facts and Fictions - Philadelphia Stickley Co. 1981 - Herbert.
-   The Illustrated Encyclopedia of Healing Remedies- C. Norman Shealy, M.D., Ph.D.
-   Yoga- A Method for Longevity - Thich Thien Thanh, Ph. D.
-   Handbook of Chinese Herbs and Formulas I & II, Thuong Truc Acupuncture.
-   The Book of the Moon - The Book of the Sun - Tom Folley.
-   Wheels of Life - A User's Guide to The Chakra System- Anodea Judith.
-   Planets in Our Solar System- Earth - Major Planets- Galaxy- Electromagnetic Spectrum- Atom and Atomic Theory - Astronomy- Models of the Universe - Microsoft Encarta Encyclopedia 1997.

MUSIC

A MOTHER'S LOVE
Words by: Angeline Lan Doan
Music by: Judy Mombleau

C   G
DUST AND LIGHT, SEPERATION AND REUNION

F   G
HOW IMMENSE A MOTHER'S LOVE IS,
  F G
ALL FOR HER

C   F G   C
CHILDREN, ALL FOR HER CHILDREN.

C   G
BLOOD AND MILK TO FORM AN
      F
ADULT, A MOTHER'S LOVE

    G   F
LIKE A PRECIOUS GEM, EXCEEDS
  G   C
EVERYTHING…

CHORUS

F
A MOTHER'S LOVE COMES FROM
C
BLOOD AND FLESH,

DIM G   C
WILL NEVER END.

AM   **EM**
BRIGHT LIGHT OF MIND, WITH MOTHER'S BLOOD

            DM   **G**
AND NOURISHING MILK, HELP THEM
                              G7
BECOME GREAT MEN,

F
WITH CREATIVE TALENTS,

   C
EVOLVING FOREVER

DM   G
IN OUR UNIVERSE…

C   **G**
ALL MOTHER'S LOVE IS THE FIRE THAT WARMS,

F   **G**
NATURE AND BRINGS ABOUT GOOD GROWN-UPS

F   **G**   **C**
MY LOVE FOR YOU IS FOREVER…

```
F          G          C
MY LOVE FOR YOU IS FOREVER...

F          G          C
MY LOVE FOR YOU IS FOREVER.
```

HEART

Words by: Angeline Lan Doan
Music by: Judy Mombleau

G   D
EVERYTHING BEGINS WITH THE
  EM
HEART.

  C   G AM
IT HELPS ACHIEVE HARMONY AND
 D
EQUALITY.

G   D
EVERYTHING BEGINS WITH THE
  EM
HEART.

  C   G AM
IT HELPS ACHIEVE HARMONY
  D
AMONG US.

C   G
WE CAN DISTINGUISH RIGHT FROM WRONG

AM   **G**
THANKS TO THE HIGHEST HEART, WE'RE STRONG.

C   **G**
IT LIGHTS A LAMP IN OUR MIND; TO
AM
REACH THE GOALS,

    D
TO REACH THE GOALS, OF OUR GOD,
G C   D   G
OF OUR GOD.

REPEAT.

A Letter from the Heart
To My Children:

Elise Lan Tran
Duke Ngoc Tran
Aileen Ngoc Tran

Also specially addressed to young generations all over the world.

My dear children,

First of all, the love I have been giving you since your first day in life is the sincerest one, which comes from the bottom of my heart. This endless feeling will never disappear in my mind. It is expressed by my wish for you to become good people, good to yourself, to society and to your country.

The pages in this simple book are where my body and soul are preserved. Even when I am near or faraway from you, they will forever stay with you.

My children, you should consider the content of this book the yardstick to raise your level of moral, intellectual education and your creative mind to build for yourselves a noble life.

I will be completely happy when I know that you understand my thoughts clearly and try your best to improve yourselves intellectually and morally.

My sincere wish is that of a loving mother who wants you to set a good example for other people.

This great spring of love and even this body of mine are reserved for you, my children, through a rough and unsteady life.

I wish that my saddest tears would transform into sweet dew that would bring about hope to you and give birth to only good seeds so that:

"Suffering will become happiness
Impurity will become purity
And bad smell will become wafting aroma."

Since you have learned from my life's practical experience, I am certain that you will be able to use it as a means to serve yourselves and society just as "sand will become precious stones".

Once you have understood my recommendations and my love, you should apply them to your life when you grow up.

"Dust and light
Separation and reunion
How immense
A mother's love is.
All for her children,
Blood and milk,
To form an adult
A mother's love
Like an invaluable gem
Exceeds everything.
A mother's love
Which comes from
Blood and flesh
Will never end.
Bright light of the mind
With mother's blood
And nourishing milk
Helps world's humans
Become great men
With creative talents
Evolving forever
In out universe,
A mother's love
Is the fire
That warms nature
And brings about
Good grown-ups
My love for you
Is forever."

Your dear mother
Angeline Lan Doan (Hong Ngoc Chau)

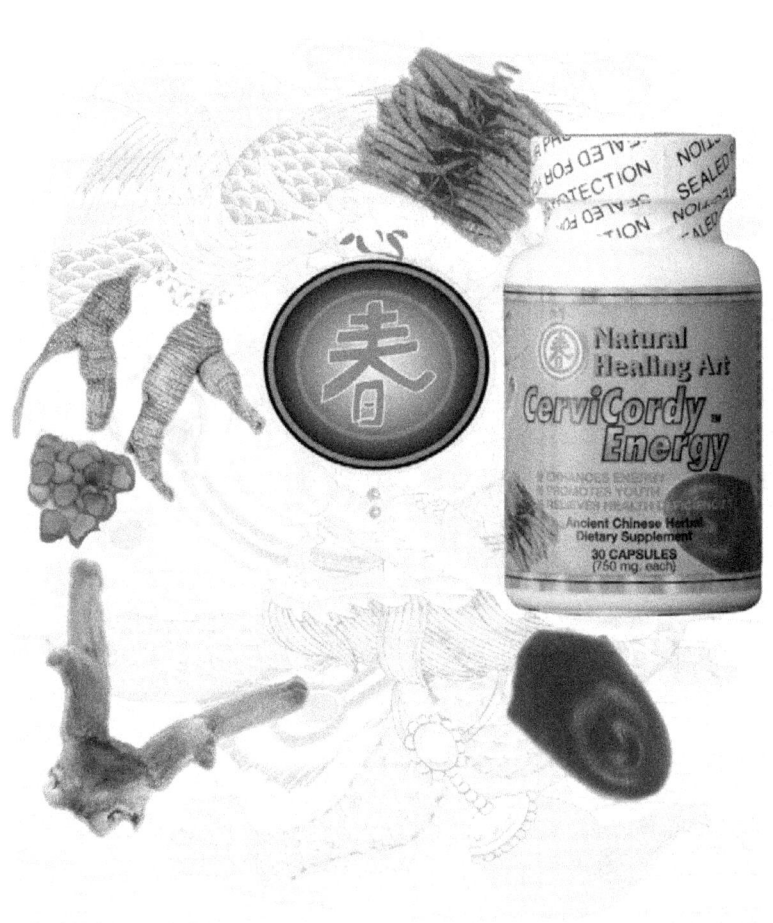

HUMANITY

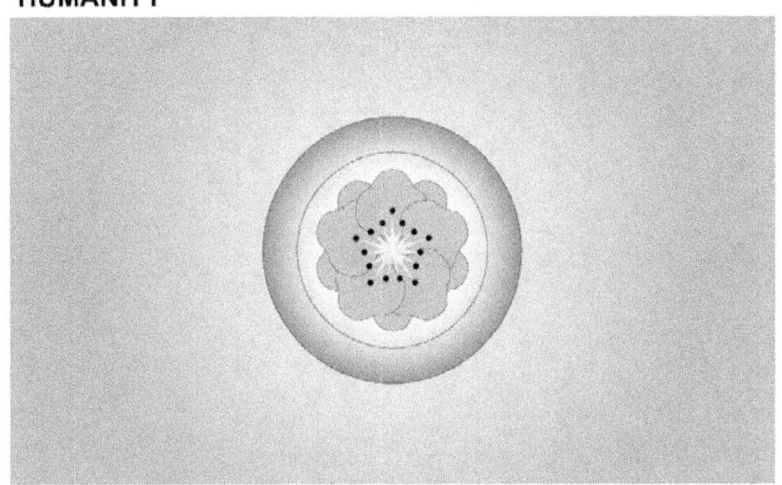

"*Cherries blooming are to welcome Spring,*
My heart is deeply moved, nourishing the spirit of Spring,
Will lead us to paradise, and bring us happiness forever..."